An Edwardian
Housewife's
Companion

Rowena Davison
with Reuben Davison

First published in 2009. A catalogue record for this book is available from the British Library

ISBN 978-1-844258-14-7

Published by Haynes Publishing, Sparkford, Yeovil, Somerset BA22 7JJ, UK

Tel: 01963 442030 Fax: 01963 440001 Int. tel: +44 1963 442030 Int. fax: +44 1963 440001

E-mail: sales@haynes.co.uk Website: www.haynes.co.uk

Haynes North America Inc., 861 Lawrence Drive, Newbury Park, California 91320, USA

All images © Mirrorpix

Creative Director: Kevin Gardner

Packaged for Haynes by Green Umbrella Publishing

Printed and bound by J F Print Ltd., Sparkford, Somerset

An Edwardian
Housewife's Companion

A Guide for
THE PERFECT HOME

~ *An Edwardian* Housewife's Companion ~

Contents

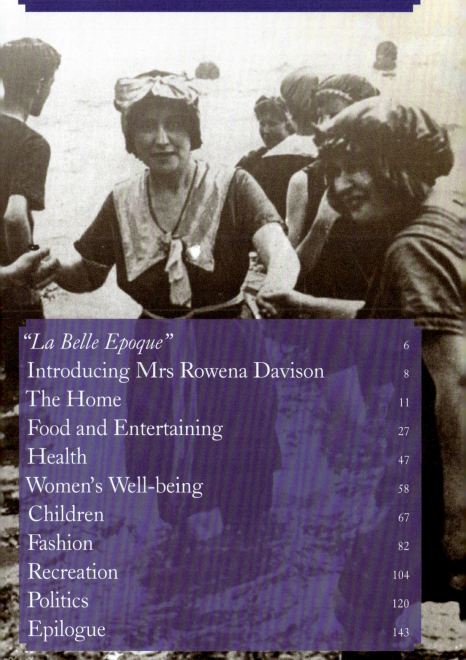

"La Belle Epoque" 6
Introducing Mrs Rowena Davison 8
The Home 11
Food and Entertaining 27
Health 47
Women's Well-being 58
Children 67
Fashion 82
Recreation 104
Politics 120
Epilogue 143

"La Belle Epoque"

Edward VII became King on 22 January 1901 following the death of his mother, Queen Victoria. Aged 59 and the longest heir apparent in British history, he was soon to give his name to an era.

Unlike the later Victorian period, when the royal court and society at large followed the Queen in her long period of mourning for her husband's early death, the Edwardian period is usually remembered for ostentatious displays of wealth and social climbing. But it was also a dramatic period for all levels of society. The Suffragette movement was battling to get votes for women, Acts of Parliament were passed to alleviate the suffering of children, and Irish Home Rule was being debated.

Our own image of Edwardian society is generally coloured by television series such as *The Forsyte Saga*, *Lillie*, *Upstairs Downstairs* and, most recently, *The Edwardian Country House*. For many, this era is seen as a "golden age" – a frequently used phrase in writing about this period.

"The lost golden age . . . all the more radiant because it is on the other side of the huge black pit of war." – J B Priestley

Prince Albert Edward was born in Buckingham Palace on 9 November 1841. Affectionately known as "Bertie" to his family and officially titled the Prince of Wales from December 1841, he decided to use the name Edward instead of his given name, Albert Edward, since *"he did not want to undervalue the name of Albert or diminish the status of his father with whom among Royalty the name Albert should stand alone".*

As the eldest son of Queen Victoria and Prince Albert he was brought up to take on his inevitable role as monarch. With this in mind Prince Albert supervised his son's education. Edward was encouraged to travel and undertook a number of overseas tours representing the Queen.

On 10 March 1863 the Prince was married to Princess Alexandra of Denmark, at St George's Chapel, Windsor. Edward, however, was a great socialite, preferring the company of actors and actresses, singers and dancers, people we would describe today as celebrities. Edward was later to be labelled a "playboy", his numerous affairs leading to the highly embarrassing episode of Sir Charles Mordaunt threatening to name him as co-respondent in his forthcoming divorce case. Whatever the truth behind the many accusations and claims of illegitimate children, they did little for Edward's credibility or standing within the Royal Family. But perhaps his most famous liaison was with Alice Keppel, whose great-granddaughter is Camilla Parker Bowles, Duchess of Cornwall, now married to the current Prince of Wales and heir apparent.

With his extensive travels both in the United Kingdom and overseas reported and photographed in the newspapers, Edward began to set trends, particularly in fashion. His love of country sports helped to popularise the wearing of tweeds and the Norfolk jacket, and he was instrumental in what was seen as the radical shift from the traditional white tie to a black tie with a dinner jacket. We also owe the traditional Sunday lunch to Edward's influence.

But the aim of this book is less to shed light on Edward himself than on "his" age, and in particular to show how an Edwardian lady was expected to conduct herself – what she should wear, what she and her family should eat and how she should maintain the standards expected of her. Etiquette was crucial in this era, and failure to adhere to its strict rules brought an immediate accusation of social inferiority – an intolerable label for the Edwardian middle classes. All this we shall see through the eyes of one particular lady, one who embodies many of the characteristic features of Edwardian society.

King Edward VII, 1900.

Introducing Mrs Rowena Davison

Let me introduce myself. I am Rowena Davison, 42 years old, married to Charles Davison. Our twin children, Edward and Emily, are both still at school.

We have been fortunate to move away from the centre of Bradford and purchase a new house in Heaton. As both our businesses have expanded – Charles owns and runs a woollen mill in the city, and I run a dressmaking and milliner's business – we felt that a move was in order. The area is more affluent and we now have a property with a large garden where the children can play, and Lister Park is only a few hundred yards away: we sometimes take a walk around the lake there or visit the Botanical Gardens.

We employ three staff to help in the house – a housekeeper, who lives in, a cook, who comes in every day, and a young girl who does the general housework and chores. She is the daughter of one of my staff.

Many people would say we lead a comfortable life, but this doesn't mean I don't have to keep my eye on all our expenditure. We like to entertain regularly (and for people in our position this is of course expected), so planning the menus and guest lists go hand in hand with the administration needed to run my own business, which I have been doing for five years now.

My shop on Manningham Lane, Bradford, 1905.

My clients are all in a similar position to myself, being the wives of businessmen, bank managers and shop owners, though I have two theatrical clients as well. All my "ladies" are fashion conscious and want to keep up to date with the latest designs from Paris and across the world, so I quite often attend the shows in Paris and elsewhere to see what I should be buying and making in my workshop. The staff I employ are all expert seamstresses and are able to create the designs which, at the prices of the major fashion houses, may be out of reach of all but the most wealthy.

I regularly read the newspapers (despite the fact that my husband finds this somewhat "unnecessary"), and I take an active interest in politics, an area that gives me great concern at this time. It appears quite unseemly the way some women are carrying on with their campaign for women's votes. Charles has no time whatsoever for these "vulgar women", as he often describes them. I do have some sympathy for them, although their means are at times a little dubious – but how else are we women to be taken seriously?

Since Edward came to the throne he has certainly made an impression on our society. He seems so much more lively than our dear Queen Victoria, and, it has to be said, a very stylish gentleman – and definitely at ease with the ladies.

In the following pages I will give you some advice on the daily problems of how best to look after your children and what to wear (one really cannot underestimate the importance of dressing correctly, especially if one is going to a party or invited to the country). I shall also be offering hints and ideas that I have learnt in household management, including some of my favourite recipes, and passing on some of the tips that help keep my complexion radiant and bright and the family in good health. And along the way we shall take a look at the stars of the stage and music hall, whom we all adore.

Finally, there is so much to impart about treating one's staff correctly – an area of extreme importance if one is to maintain standards within the household – so I will include guidance on this matter too.

Mrs Rowena Davison

The Home

House styles began to change rapidly through the Edwardian era. Influences from the Arts and Crafts movement were widely employed, along with a return to Georgian styles. The home became less cluttered and there was a desire for space and fresh air. Stores began selling furniture that could be purchased on credit terms, a new proposition for many families, not just the poorer ones. An increasing number of houses had electricity, which allowed for new devices such as the vacuum cleaner and the telephone.

Tyrrell Street, Bradford, 1908.

It gives me particular pleasure that we can now give a name to our house, instead of calling it simply "Number 42". We chose "The Elms", which (rather foolish, I know) gave me a greater sense of our increasing status.

The house is much larger than our previous one, and being new shows many of the latest styles. There is an abundance of turned woodwork for the verandas and a small balcony with French doors outside our first floor bedroom. Some of the most exquisite stained glass is used in the windows and doors, and there is a pretty mosaic pathway up to the front door, which is continued into the hallway; even the porch walls are tiled. Inside, the hallway has parquet flooring, which looks beautiful when polished.

To help me in the task of setting up house I kept a journal of all the advertisements I had found in the newspapers – what was fashionable and what people in our position were buying. My favourite store is Wolfe & Hollander's in Leeds, who offer a remarkable array of ideas to furnish the entire home. They have whole rooms laid out with everything you could possibly want.

Having been fortunate to buy this new house I wanted as much as possible to be new, fresh and up to date. Charles and I did not always agree on this. I said it was time to get rid of as much of our old furniture as possible. He didn't see the need to spend unnecessarily (he never did), but I insisted we could afford it now we were more successful and explained that "quality cannot be bought cheaply" and a shabby home reflected a shabby family; "time and money spent improving and furnishing the home was time and money well spent" (I didn't admit that I had remembered these phrases from the stores' advertising literature.)

Wolfe & Hollander's also offers payments by instalments. If

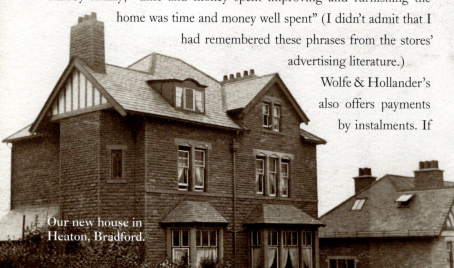

Our new house in Heaton, Bradford.

we were going to maintain our standing I felt it necessary to investigate this opportunity. More and more stores are beginning to offer this facility. In the beginning this was seen by many as something only the poorer classes did; but now it is regarded as something everyone can consider.

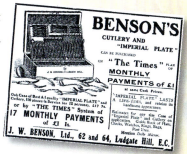

All we had to do was visit the store, select the furniture we required and tell them we wished to pay by instalment. It was quite simple – except that my husband felt it somewhat beneath us to be requesting credit. However, after much discussion he agreed that this was a suitable means, and so I listed what we needed and placed an order.

First I chose the furniture for the bedroom, a beautiful fumed oak suite consisting of a wardrobe, dressing chest, marble washstand and a set of chairs to match. The wardrobe had particularly fine copper panelling. We have kept our old bed since this was a gift from Charles's parents on our marriage.

The dining room was my next concern. We regularly entertain so we needed a large dining table; a sideboard on which to place the food before serving; somewhere for the drinks and glasses to be stored; and possibly a display cabinet for our finer porcelain and china (the everyday plates and cutlery are kept in the kitchen).

A special joy to me with our new home is the "boudoir", a room purely for my own use. Such a room is becoming *de rigueur* for people in our position. I can retire there to write my letters or do some needlework. It is also a place of relaxation to recover from the rigours of daily life. My husband has his study, so he too can retire and attend to business correspondence or read the papers and partake of a pipe, something I am far happier him doing in his own room.

A mixed blessing has been the introduction of electricity. We have until now been used to gas, which, although a chore to maintain, provides a softer light than this rather harsh electric glare we now have, which is at times not very flattering to one's complexion. I shall not relate all the details

ASTER
MARINE ENGINES

ASTER
45/50 HP Type 47 PF4

"No madam, you will not need one of
these for your new kitchen ."

of the kitchen but I must mention the bathroom. We decided to install one of the new baths that had just become available. The hot water was provided by a gas-powered geyser. Whilst it seemed a good idea and we had to consider these new inventions, both Charles and I really preferred to wash in our rooms as we had always done.

The children's rooms are simply furnished with the necessary items such as a bed, wardrobe and a set of drawers. Each of their rooms has a small sink as well, so they can wash.

We have kept the wooden floors and use an array of rugs we have brought from our first house. The bathroom has a new linoleum floor, which is very practical and very easy for the housekeeper to clean.

It has taken us well over a year to fully furnish the house but it has been worth the wait. Our friends are very impressed. We have parties and dinners for friends and Charles's business colleagues. Moving to this larger property has also given us the room to take on further staff in the near future, if we wish.

The garden is also larger than our last. We occasionally sit out as a family and even enjoy a meal outside when the weather is fine. Since we have settled our interior designs and requirements I am able to take an active interest in the garden – which is just as well because there was much to do and I have read as much as I can by way of the flowers and shrubs we might have. A local tradesman has laid a path so we can have access to all the areas and the borders. I was particularly keen on having lots of trellises, so that we can grow a variety of roses and hollyhocks, though my pride and joy are the dazzling displays of lupins and delphiniums.

I have seen in the magazines that one can obtain specially made outdoor furniture made of wicker or cane, but Charles thinks this extravagant and suggests we simply move a table and chairs outside when we need them. He is also doubtful about sitting in the garden at all. A rather startling but fascinating addition to our garden is a motor lawn mower. Charles was so nervous of using his machine that the job has been left to our part-time gardener.

Bradford, with its abundance of mills and factories and its situation in a topographical bowl, is not generally noted for its clean air. But I assure you it is at the forefront of healthy living for schoolchildren. My husband and I make a number of charitable donations to the Open Air School on the outskirts of the city. Here the children are taught outside when the weather is fine and, when it is not, they move to inside classrooms which are open to the elements – all extremely invigorating for the children.

Servants

The treatment of servants is always close to my mind and an area where one cannot afford to make mistakes. Whilst we only have three servants at present, I am sure we shall be employing more in the coming months. Below I outline some general rules in this matter, based on my reading and personal observations.

- ❖ All family members should maintain appropriate relationships with the staff.
- ❖ Servants will work directly to the family and a trusting and respectful relationship should be established.

- ❖ While the housemaids clean the house during the day, they should take every care and attention never to be observed doing their duty. If by chance you do meet, you should expect them to "give way" to you by standing still and averting their gaze whilst you walk past, leaving them unnoticed. By not acknowledging them, you will spare them the shame of explaining their presence.
- ❖ The butler should be addressed by his surname.
- ❖ The housemaid should be given the title of "Missus".
- ❖ A ladies maid will be given the title "Miss", regardless of whether she is single or married; however, addressing her by her Christian name is acceptable.
- ❖ A tutor should be addressed by the title of "Mister".
- ❖ It is very much the custom in the older houses that, when entering into new service, lower servants adopt a name given to them by their masters. You may follow this tradition and rename certain members of your staff. Common names for matching footmen are James and John, whilst Emma is popular for housemaids.
- ❖ If you have a large household, it is not expected that you trouble yourself to remember the names of all your staff. Indeed, in order to avoid obliging you to converse with them, lower servants will endeavour to make themselves invisible to you. As such they should not be acknowledged.

Then, of course, are the rules that the servants themselves must obey. Some of these are as follows:

Servants' Rules

- ❖ Never let your voice be heard by the ladies and gentlemen of the house.
- ❖ Always "give room" if you meet one of your employers or betters on the stairs.
- ❖ Always stand still when being spoken to by a lady and look at the person speaking to you.
- ❖ Never take the initiative in addressing ladies or gentlemen.
- ❖ Never offer an opinion to your employers, nor even say goodnight.

- ❖ Never talk to another servant in the presence of your mistress.
- ❖ Never call from one room to another.
- ❖ Only the butler may answer the door bell.
- ❖ No gambling, oaths or abusive language is allowed.
- ❖ The female staff are forbidden from smoking.
- ❖ Any maid found fraternising with a member of the opposite sex will be dismissed without a hearing.
- ❖ The hall door is to be finally closed at half past 10 o'clock every night.
- ❖ Any breakages or damage to the house will be deducted from wages.

(You will find more of these rules in the next chapter, especially those pertaining to dining and dining etiquette.)

The jobs of servants are many and varied, and so to avoid any confusion or misunderstanding I feel that these should be elaborated upon, too. Our own household is small and therefore a butler is not necessary, but if you are fortunate to be living in a much larger household then you will need to know about all the staff positions that need to be filled.

The Butler

The butler is usually the most senior member of staff, except in some of the larger houses where he might be in charge of just the dining room and possibly the wine cellar. He is responsible for the hiring and dismissing of all the other household staff, and he receives direct instruction from the master and mistress of the household as to what they require and details such as dates for entertaining or when the master might be away on business.

The Ladies Maid

The ladies maid attends only to the lady of the household. She is similar in position to the gentleman's valet (a position my husband has not yet managed to fill). She should be available from the time the lady rises to the time she finally retires to bed. She maintains the wardrobe and mends any clothing that needs attention. She is addressed usually by her first name, a privilege not normally accorded to other members of staff. The hours are long and demanding but, in compensation, she gains a higher social status and is sometimes required to travel with her mistress.

The Cook

The cook is always female. She is responsible for food preparation and the smooth and efficient running of the kitchens. Another important role is that of keeping accounts with the local merchants who supply the household. She is consulted with regard to all menus, both for the daily meals and when any entertaining is to be done. Most cooks will have worked their way up to this position from being a kitchenmaid.

The Housekeeper

The housekeeper is responsible for the cleaning and maintenance of the household. This is also considered an important position – so much so that she may be attended to by some of the junior staff. This can manifest itself in her having her room cleaned or being served in the dining hall along with the butler. Once again she is responsible to the lady of the house from whom she will receive all her instructions. Other duties might involve the hiring of junior staff.

Here in the Bradford area we have experienced some initial problems obtaining servants. As this article in a national paper pointed out:

"The type of servant girl procurable in Bradford is said to be distinctly low, her moral not over good, and her capacity often beneath contempt."

This description does not apply to our current female staff of course, who are of excellent character and who have been chosen very carefully. As I mentioned earlier, one girl is the daughter of one of my own employees, and accordingly very reliable and hard working.

The purchase of new labour-saving devices can be a contentious matter. Almost daily one reads of such new inventions – vacuum cleaners, electric irons, kettles and washing machines, and so on. I am all in favour but Charles is reluctant to purchase them because he feels we should be putting the servants out of a job.

Household Responsibilities

There is so much for the wife to do and consider when running the home. (I know this from experience, since as well as running my own business, I need to attend to my husband's needs and wishes, particularly after he has had a long and arduous day's work.)

Which woman makes the best wife?

Why, surely, beauty, artistic tendencies, smartness, count for nothing. The woman with a "grip on the situation", to use an Americanism, the woman who is ready to use every influence to secure comfort for her husband, and recompense him for the toil and labour he undergoes to make that place called "home" an abiding joy – this is the woman who makes the best wife.

The smooth running of the household is essential for all concerned; marriage and family are not to be taken lightly and there are responsibilities to be upheld. Through my reading I have learnt a great deal about how a husband and wife should conduct themselves both within and without the house. I offer some of those observations here so that readers may also benefit from this wisdom.

The Wife's Responsibilities

- ❖ Never should a wife display her best conduct, her accomplishments, her smiles and her best nature exclusively away from home.
- ❖ Be careful in your purchases. Let your husband know what you buy and that you have wisely expended your money.
- ❖ Beware of bickering about little things. Your husband returns from his labours with his mind absorbed in business. With his employees he is used to being obeyed and may well forget this difference between work and home. Make home so charming that he will gladly yield all management of it to you.

- Be careful of your conduct and language. A husband is largely restrained by the chastity, purity and refinement of his wife. A lowering of dignity, a looseness of expression and vulgarity of words may greatly lower the standard of the husband's purity of speech and morals.

The Husband's Responsibilities

- A very grave concern has the man assumed in marriage. Doting parents have confided to his care the welfare of a loved daughter, and a trusting woman has risked all her future happiness in his keeping. Largely it will depend on him whether her pathway shall be strewn with thorns or roses.

- Do not be dictatorial in the family circle. The home is the wife's province. It is her natural field of labour. It is her right to govern and

dictate its interior management. You should not interfere with duties which legitimately belong to her.

❖ If a dispute arises, dismiss the subject with a kind word. It is a glorious achievement to master one's own temper. If you discover your wife is wrong, she will gladly, in her cooler moments, acknowledge the fault.

❖ Establish your income for the coming year and ascertain what the household expenses will be and then set aside a weekly sum, which should be regularly and invariably paid to the wife at a stated time. Let this sum be even more than enough so that the wife can pay bills and have the satisfaction besides of accumulating a fund of her own with which she can exercise a spirit of independence in the bestowal of charity, the purchase of a gift, or any article she may desire.

To follow the advice given here will produce a strong and lasting relationship. There are, however, a few other aspects that are worth considering if a marriage is to be successful. Here are some sound principles taken from an article I read recently in the *Daily Mirror*:

Marry a person whom you have known long enough to be sure of his or her worth, if not personally, at least by reputation.

Marry a person who is your equal in social position. If there is a difference let the husband be superior to the wife. It is difficult for a wife to love and honour a person she is compelled to look down upon.

Marry a person of similar religious beliefs and convictions. It is equally disagreeable to the gentle, mild and sweet disposition to be united with a cold, heartless, grasping, avaricious, quarrelsome person.

The wife, confident in her husband's strength and wisdom, will thus implicitly yield to his protective care. And thus, both will be happy – he in exercising the prerogatives which belong naturally to the guardian and protector; and she in her confidence, love and respect for her companion, whom she can implicitly trust.

In Conclusion:

❖ Let the rebuke be followed by a kiss

❖ Do not require a request to be repeated

- Never should both be angry at the same time
- Angry words be answered only with a kiss
- Make your criticism in the most loving manner possible
- Bestow your warmest sympathies in each other's trials

Adherence to these principles will ensure a happy and loving household at all times.

I always strive to reach the standards expected of a woman in my position and appreciate any advice offered to me. No woman should be without a copy of Dorothy Peel's *How to Keep House*, an excellent guide to all one needs to know in this field.

> Dorothy offers advice such as this:
>
> *Men do appreciate eating and the general pleasures of the table, and that woman who can, in addition to her other graces, attend to the wants of a man in this special direction is the woman who will succeed as a wife. Men, because of their strenuous life, certainly do need proper food; and women, to keep their strength for their great "small tasks", should appreciate more fully than they do the necessity for keeping brain and body supplied with energy, which only is stored by eating sensible foods. It is the forethought that the wife may show in preparing such a valuable addition to the meal that will be appreciated by the wearied husband.*

Visitors and Visiting

To observe the correct manners is essential at all times while entertaining. When you pay a social visit yourself, your first thought must be to greet your host or hostess on arrival. If you are entertaining a large number of guests you should always remain near the door and do not forget to make all the necessary introductions.

When visitors arrive, depending on whether they are family or close friends, strict etiquette needs to be observed. Criticism of other family members or acquaintances, for example, is not to be tolerated, nor are comments on your host's children or staff. To do this would display a

My husband's mill on the outskirts of Bradford.

distinct sign of *ill-breeding*. A simple rule is not to do or say anything that will prove disagreeable or cause ill-feeling. It is also wise to circulate at all times, so as not to offend any person with undue or insufficient attention.

On formal occasions it is usually the lady of the house who receives the visitors or guests, though she may be accompanied by her husband. In some houses the butler may well announce those arriving at a party. In this case, you may then introduce your guests around the room. If guests arrive whilst you are seated you are to stand immediately to greet them and welcome them to your home.

If you yourself are visiting, always make sure to be punctual; and if you find you cannot attend word must be sent immediately – with up to six postal deliveries a day a card may be sent with ease. You might like to consider using one of the illustrated postcards which are proving very popular at the moment.

You should also be aware of the length of your stay. Always be conscious of your host's state of mind and be sure not to overstay. Good manners decree that you will not be asked to leave even if you have become tiresome. When you do decide to leave, make your departure immediate: do not dally.

If you have made an unannounced visit and there are already guests at the house, announce yourself formally and stay only a short time, explaining that your visit is only to be brief.

Arrivals and departures for visiting and entertaining are always aided by a written invitation, indicating times guests are expected to arrive and (importantly for some), their expected departure times.

If any of your guests should spend the night in your household after a party then you should be careful to instruct your staff (if you are so fortunate) to observe your guests at all times and make sure every comfort is extended to them, not only during the party but on arrival and afterwards. Make sure warm baths are offered and clean, freshly laundered towels are available at all times. If guests are to remain in their rooms then servants should visit at least twice a day to see if they require anything.

Most of our own friends and family live within the city, so we rarely need to accommodate guests. But as we have a larger house these days I am looking forward to having a few select friends to stay for the weekend, and I suppose it is about time we asked Charles's parents to stay; now that they have retired to the east coast I feel it is my duty to do so.

Food and Entertaining

For the wealthier classes, food and entertaining played a prominent role in daily life in this period. Entertaining on a grand scale could involve the preparation of meals consisting of 12 courses or more, with all that that implies in terms of servants, upstairs and downstairs. For the poor, on the other hand, mealtimes were a matter of making what little you could afford go as far as possible.

Open fronted butchers shop, 1909.

You may like to follow my example and collect recipes that can be passed on to the cook. I have found most of my favourites from newspapers such as the *Daily Mirror*, the *Bradford Daily Telegraph* and the *Yorkshire Observer*, though occasionally a guest will suggest a recipe she has found particularly pleasing.

In most households not all meals are grand affairs, and so your recipe collection must reflect this. In our family of four we do not have a formal meal every evening, but Charles does like to dine formally at weekends, when we dress for dinner and on occasion also invite guests. From time to time we have brought in a caterer, but this can prove very expensive and in our case I feel that using our own staff is far more satisfactory.

Here is a menu common to many households:

Breakfast: *Porridge, Sardines on Toast, Curried Eggs, Grilled Cutlets, Bread and Butter, Honey, Coffee or Chocolate*

Lunch: *Sauté of Kidneys, Mashed Potatoes, Rolled Ox Tongue, Macaroni au Gratin*

Tea: *Hot Potato Scones, Coconut Rocks, Madeira Cake, Bread and Butter, Toast*

Dinner: *Oyster Patties, Sirloin Steak, Braised Celery, Roast Goose, Potato Scallops, Vanilla Soufflé*

In some establishments it is not unknown to add a pre-bed snack of cold goose and a glass of Madeira.

The times of meals can be decided upon by the family and the business of the day. Breakfast in our household is always at 7.30am sharp. I am not one for a large breakfast, and will normally have tea or coffee and perhaps a little toast; toast must be served hot. It must not be left to go cold since it then becomes quite unpalatable – as I am at pains to point out to cook. Charles, on the other hand, likes to take a breakfast of porridge followed by eggs, meat and possibly a little fruit to finish off. He always takes tea with his meal, never coffee, which he says leaves a bitter taste in the mouth for the rest of the day.

Lunch (or luncheon, as some people prefer to say) may also be formal or informal, served between 12.30pm and 1.30pm. Among the most popular dishes for luncheon are oysters, beef steak, fish, omelettes and a selection of salads. If you are entertaining guests then it is correct to have the servants hand the various dishes to the table (whereas when there are no guests it is quite acceptable to dispense with any formality and serve yourself). If you wish to keep things less formal then you can encourage guests to enter the dining room individually, not arm in arm as they would do for dinner.

The table should be laid with a white tablecloth and great attention should be paid to serving the courses. The sweets may be laid on the table but vegetables must always be served from the sideboard, and cold meats must be served by the hostess. You may like to give your lady guests a little memento of the occasion, perhaps a small bouquet of flowers.

Afternoon tea is a particular joy of mine, and Charles and I try to hold a small reception two or three times a month. These do not have to be formal occasions, and the range of food is substantially reduced to simple sandwiches and biscuits or fancy cakes. Under no circumstances is wine to be served, though punch is one of our special favourites, and lemonade is usually very popular in the summer months.

Since Charles and I tend not to entertain on a grand scale, these afternoon tea receptions are wonderful. I am told that in the larger houses musicians are engaged and the room darkened to add to the ambience – a little unnecessary, we find.

When we entertain we invite between three and five guests. As soon as a date has been arranged I take time with cook to draw up a suitable menu, possibly something I may have

read about and copied out for just such an occasion. I like to start with a suitable decoration

for the centre of the table. My favourite, now we have a garden, is to cut some roses and place them in a long copper trough to be placed in the centre of the table. I then add a few more in smaller vases around the table. I am ever conscious of the household expenses and try not to spend unwisely or carelessly. Below is an example of one of the menus cook and I drew up:

Cucumber purée
Whiting à la Reformé
Chicken creams
Roast lamb
Potatoes
Peas
Sardine toasts
Iced fruit salad

The dessert in this menu was particularly appealing as I took it upon myself to be rather creative in its presentation, using half a grapefruit, hollowed out to form little cups. If you don't have access to grapefruit then pineapple or melon will do.

If you are fortunate enough to have a freezer, this dish may be frozen. I stood the grapefruit halves in a large biscuit tin and packed them with plenty of chipped ice and rough salt. For those of you with an interest in the cost of this menu then you may be surprised to learn that £2 covered all the bills; both cook and I were very pleased. All in all the dinner was a great success, and I was able to offer a small lunch on the following day with the remains by simply adding a little more fish.

For a slighter grander occasion, you may wish to include appetisers. Here is a description of King Edward's favourite hors-d'oeuvres:

Oysters in Aspic

A dozen oysters, a little aspic jelly, one chilli, one small truffle, croûtes of

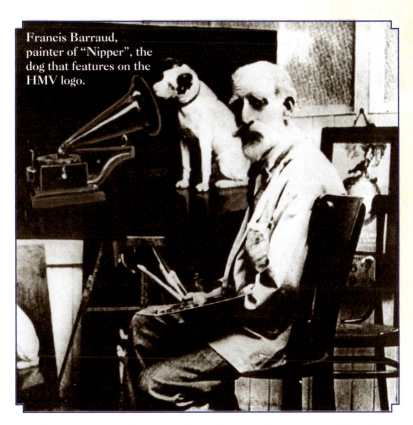

Francis Barraud, painter of "Nipper", the dog that features on the HMV logo.

bread or toast. Melt the aspic jelly and coat each oyster carefully. Leave it to set. With a very small cutter stamp out some small dots of chilli and truffle, dip each in the melted aspic, then arrange in alternate colours around the oysters. Place each oyster on a crouton, arrange them on a glass dish or plate and garnish with a little chervil or parsley.

Harlequin Croûtes

Tiny rounds of hot buttered toast, thin strips of tongue, gherkin or truffle. Arrange the strips to form a trellis over each piece of toast, blending the three colours prettily. Send them to table on lace papers.

It must be remembered that these are appetisers, to be served at the beginning of the meal, and are intended only to stimulate the appetite: they must not be rich and must not be composed of any ingredients used in the dishes of the main menu. If you wish to emulate these dishes you may prefer a simpler and more substantial recipe. Charles's favourite is:

A loin of mutton, cleaned from the strings and skin, the same quantity of kidney fat, and double quantity of oysters, bearded and wiped dry. Chop them all together, season well and rub them with flour to the size of sausages and fry them in butter or good frying fat.

For those who can afford a little more then I highly recommend Croûtes of Caviare. These are small rounds of toast spread with a little caviare and two or three olives. They are simply made: butter the toast then spread a thin layer of caviare, stone and halve the olives and place cut side down on each croûte. Garnish the croûtes with a sprig of parsley and arrange them on lace paper.

It is so important to encourage young ladies to take an interest in cooking and the preparation and planning of meals – after all, these are skills they will need when they marry. I certainly prepare my own daughter for these tasks. And I am pleased to say that in Bradford a school competition is held to encourage girls to improve their cooking skills. Each girl is given a choice of food to prepare, which I have included here:

Vegetable soup, toast
Toad in the Hole
Fried liver and bacon
Baked fish
Hot pot
Apple dumplings
Ginger pudding and sauce
Fig pudding
Stewed fruit and syrup
Fruit tart
Rice pudding

It was rather unnerving to have my own daughter return home anxious to show me how to prepare these dishes; it was also rather unsettling for cook. But it showed me that I must assist the single girl and offer some help and ideas. Some girls have so little time for cooking, and need guidance as to the preparation of suitably healthy foods.

Fruits, vegetables and nuts are essential for any growing woman – and those which have been sun-dried are the most nutritious. The following piece of advice might not be to everyone's taste:

"Among bachelor girls who do not find time enough to cook their meals, what are known as un-fired food is the present craze. Those who have servants at their command, as a rule, prefer the ordinary type of menu, but even a few gourmets are being rescued from the diet they have patronised for years.

Her dinner is heralded by a course of gymnastics in front of the window in order that she may be filled with plenty of air to help her digest her food. Then the first course of any meal will be eaten in front of the window, and consists of deep breathing and deep swallowing, for air must be swallowed with every breath that is taken. This is called the 'air-bath' and is never omitted from this form of diet."

You will no doubt make up your own minds as to the efficacy of such an activity, but let it be said that I have never witnessed any girl partaking in this activity. This piece concludes that there were other advantages to this kind of diet:

"Though un-fired food has its drawbacks, it also has advantages, particularly among bachelor girls and women whose servant difficulties are many."

I presume this refers to the difficulty one can encounter in finding servants, so that looking after oneself can be beneficial to one's well-being. It may be not insignificant, however, that this advice was followed by an advert for the recruiting of suitable and trustworthy staff.

Since healthy eating is becoming more and more talked about, you will find many new ideas on the matter in this book. Even the newspapers are beginning to promote new ways of eating and trying to encourage people to be reasonable in their eating habits. Adverts such as the one below appear regularly, offering new, healthier products.

> Healthy Crusade against Animal Butter and Lard.
> *Animal fats are being ousted by pure vegetable butter.*
> *Butter, lard and all animal fats are being superseded by a safe and hygienic vegetable product called "Palmine", which is a pure, wholesome and economical cooking butter made in England from the natural fat of the coconut.*

Even the King's physician, Sir Francis Laking, offers advice on the health benefits of dried currants:

"They are so full of brain and body building properties that they should be used daily. They are chief amongst the more valuable food at men's command."

Mealtime Etiquette

Good manners are essential in all areas of life, but particularly at table; and if one is to be seen as a good hostess adherence to etiquette is essential.

Greediness should not be indulged in. Indecision must be avoided.

Do not take up one piece and lay it down in favour of another, or hesitate.

Never allow a servant to fill up your glass with wine that you do not wish to drink. You can check him by touching the rim of your glass.

Never use a napkin in place of a handkerchief for wiping your forehead, face or nose!

Everything that can be cut with a knife should be eaten with the fork alone.

It is not in good taste to urge your guests to eat, nor load the plates with food against their inclination.

Do not toy with your knife or play with your fingers upon the table. Do not draw imaginary lines upon the tablecloth.

(I regret to say that the last instruction is one my dear Charles seems to forget on many occasions.)

Also of crucial importance is the behaviour of servants at mealtimes. As in all areas of their working lives, there are standards to be maintained.

These include:
❖ The wearing of gloves when serving food (or, alternatively, they may use a napkin, the essential point being that no part of the hand touches the plate).

- Hands and nails are to be perfectly clean.
- Coughing and breathing loudly are to be discouraged and they should go about their business quietly.

I would also advise that the following table manners are the most appropriate to follow:

- Spread the napkin over your knees, never tuck it in or fasten it at the neck.
- After use fold your napkin.
- Hold the fork in the palm of your left hand. If it is held in the right hand the prongs should face upwards.
- Do not bend over the plate with your head too low and never have your back turned away from the person next to you.
- Never use a spoon to eat vegetables; always use a fork.
- Never decline the last piece of bread if offered; it might be seen as a suggestion that the hostess had not provided enough.
- Under no circumstances must the knife be used to place food in the mouth. It is there for cutting only.

Of equal importance to a successful meal is the order in which the courses are served.

Oysters may be served to begin with. You should offer no more than five or six per person and ensure they are served extremely cold and in half of their shell, garnished with a piece of lemon.

Soup may follow. Two types are permissible, either a white and a clear soup or a white soup and a brown soup.

Fish is to follow the soup (and you must remember to lay a fish knife as well as a fork. If this hasn't been done then the use of a fork in the right hand and a small piece of bread in the other may be used).

Remember that certain sauces are served with particular fish; lobster sauce with turbot, shrimp or caper with salmon, and oyster sauce with cod.

Meat and vegetables will follow the fish. Vegetables may include asparagus, sweetcorn, artichoke or baked tomato, but never offer more than two vegetables with the one course.

The host's ability to carve is important; this is a skill that requires study and attention. It is acceptable, however, to have the meat carved away from the table and put back to look as though it has not yet been carved. (But best of all is to encourage your husband to acquire the skill of carving at the earliest opportunity.)

Game can follow the meat course and should be served with a salad which may include cheese with bread and butter. Remember the bread must always be cut very thin.

The table must then be cleared and any crumbs brushed away before dessert is served. Clearing of the crumbs may be done with a clean napkin unless you are fortunate enough to possess a crumb-scraper machine.

At last comes the dessert, which can be followed with fruit (if you are serving fruit that can stain easily, give each guest a new napkin).

QUART
SAMPLE
FREE
TO ALL
LADIES.

QUART
SAMPLE
FREE
TO ALL
LADIES.

Foster Clark's

CREAM CUSTARD

VANILLA

REAL CUSTARD

.Real, Creamy, Delicious Custard! Don't think that Foster Clark's Cream Custard is just ordinary custard. It is something quite different—something better. Eaten by itself or with stewed fruit, its wholesome excellence will appeal to all, and at once create an appreciative appetite that never tires. You have your choice of several distinct flavourings. With Foster Clark's Cream Custard packed in dainty proof tins. 6½d. will buy sufficient to make 12 quarts, enough for 36 persons. Just like it should be, and that is Foster Clark's Cream Custard!

FREE SAMPLE. —You are cordially invited to send to-day for a special quart supply of Cream Custard, which will be forwarded free of cost. Applications should be addressed to Foster Clark & Co. (Dept. 280), Maidstone, Kent. A postcard will do.

Foster Clark's
Cream Custard
12 QUARTS 6½d.

Finally, bonbons are then served before the ladies retire to the drawing room for coffee. The coffee is to be strong, black and served in tiny cups.

Many of my readers will have noted the increasing prevalence – again thanks to the influence of our King – for "service à la russe" in formal dining. This service in the Russian style favours courses being brought out in sequence; whereas the "service à la française", or service in the French style, involves all courses being served at the table at the same time, which is very impressive in appearance but somewhat impractical.

It is imperative if you are adopting this "Russian" style that you observe its rules governing the layout of each guest's place setting, or, to give it the correct name "cover".

Each guest will have a service plate on which a napkin and place card are placed, showing the name of the guest to be seated there. The cutlery must be laid out in order of usage, working from the outside in. If both fruit and salad are being served then a knife and fork must be brought to table when required since to have more than three items of cutlery laid at once is considered bad form.

Guests will be seated according to the names on the place cards and napkins will be placed on their laps. It is generally considered unacceptable to open one's napkin before the host or hostess have opened theirs. The same rule applies to the start of the meal: guests should start eating only when the hosts have begun. Similarly, one should leave the table only when a discreet signal is given by the hostess. (You would do well to be always on the alert for this, as it may at times be very hard to spot – even the merest nod of the head.) The ladies will rise first, and one should leave the dining room in the same order as you came in.

As we have seen, once the meal is finished the ladies should rise together and go to the drawing room for coffee while the men enjoy port or brandy with a cigar, and join them later. When the final course has been served the servants may retire from the dining room and any further service can be given by the gentlemen themselves.

The Serving of Drinks

Some advice about the serving of wines may be useful.

Sherry should always be decanted and may be served with the soup. You may also serve a white wine, which should not be decanted; but whichever you choose, remember to serve it cold.

Following the soup course Champagne may be served with the meat. A napkin is to be placed around the neck of the bottle to catch any spills. Once again, this must be served very cold. A useful tip is to chill the bottle for several hours before use.

A claret should be served with any game courses, and must be warm. Claret may also be served with the salad course, if separate.

Madeira wine is the best to accompany the dessert, and should be served at room temperature.

You should place a glass for each type of wine on the table, except for Madeira glasses, which should be left on the sideboard and only brought to table when it has been cleared of the previous courses and before dessert is served.

It is acceptable to offer natural water or some prefer a mineral water to your guests.

Coffee will be taken to the ladies when they have left the table.

A new fashion in drinking that is becoming very popular is the serving of cocktails – another influence from our American cousins, but generally available only in some of our smarter hotels. This is not an area in which I have much experience, but I will endeavour to offer a few recipes you might wish to try.

The Daiquiri

I am told this drink was invented by a group of mining engineers in Cuba.

You take a tall glass and fill it with cracked ice. Add a teaspoon of sugar and the juice of two limes, followed by two to three ounces of rum.

The Blue Blazer

Mix into one mug one wine glass of Scotch Whisky with one wine glass of boiling water. Heat the liquid and whilst it blazes further mix the ingredients by pouring them from one mug to another four or five times. This will give the appearance of a trail of flame! It can then be sweetened with a teaspoon of sugar and served in a small tumbler.

Flash of Lightning

Take a wine glass of brandy, half a teaspoon of gingerette, a table spoon of raspberry syrup and shake all together with ice and then strain.

Finally I offer one cocktail with a questionable name, which I hope you will not find offensive:

The Bosom Caresser

Mix together one egg, half a sherry glass of strawberry syrup and one glass of brandy. Shake well and strain.

Having a smoke before joining a shooting party.

A Royal Table

King Edward has been responsible for many influences on our dress and eating habits, and so, as an interlude, readers may like to learn one or two pieces of information I have learned about the royal table.

Surprisingly perhaps, the King cannot always rely on the best of everything; and this is particularly true of the kitchens at Windsor Castle:

"There is something piquant in the thought that while even the humblest housewife amongst us all prides herself on an up to date kitchen , the King has to be contented, when at Windsor Castle, with a vast old vaulted hall which remains perhaps the only portion of the castle that remains exactly as it was in the Middle Ages."

For state banquets at the castle a fine dinner service is used, either of gold or of silver; however, these are not the most valuable items of plate to be seen. Arranged on sideboards around the dining room is the Royal Plate, said to be worth nearly two million pounds. The highlight of this collection is the nautilus cup said to have been the work of Benvenuto Cellini. A telling contrast to this splendour is a small, silver-gilt porridge pot used by Napoleon I, which was found in his deserted travelling case after the Battle of Waterloo.

The kitchen staff at Windsor Castle comprise a master cook and three assistants, the roasting cook, apprentices, scourers, kitchenmaids, pastry maids and the rather quaintly named *"necessary woman"*. Unfortunately, I can find no reference as to the precise nature of her tasks.

Yet, as those of you with an interest in royal matters will know, Windsor Castle has a reputation for exemplary cookery and some recipes are unique to the castle. Woodcock pie has been made there for centuries and each year one is sent to every member of the Royal Family along with a Windsor Plum Pudding, wherever they are in the world.

One of the King's favourite cooks is Miss Rosa Lewis, owner of the Cavendish Hotel in Jermyn Street. Rosa has worked in a variety of kitchens, beginning her career at the home of the Comte de Paris. Her notoriety increased, however, when she went to work for Lady Randolph Churchill. It was here that the Prince of Wales became aware of her, exclaiming one time that *"Damn, she takes more pains with her cabbage than with her chicken... she gives me nothing sloppy, nothing coloured up to dribble on a man's shirt-front!"*

The King employed Rosa and her entourage for the Coronation celebrations in 1902. At this time she catered for 29 suppers for various balls and events. It was her payment for this undertaking that gave her the funds to purchase the Cavendish Hotel, which has become *the* place for the aristocracy and the wealthy to entertain, some even having a suite of rooms there.

I do not wish to openly criticise our dear King, but before he came to the throne he did much to popularise more formal dining and larger parties. When dining out you may find meals can now be unduly copious; and whilst you are not expected to partake of every course, one rarely feels comfortable afterwards (and of course our restrictive dress doesn't help matters in this respect).

Royal dining aside, the wealthy often employ a chef – a French chef is the most desirable, I am told. Dinner parties are important occasions if one's reputation is to be upheld, and everything must be approached with the utmost care and attention to detail, since one slip might be held against you for many years and will almost certainly result in invitations declining; it will also bring into question your breeding and knowledge of the finer points of life.

If a large number of guests are being entertained, say up to 20, then a vast number of pieces of china, glass and silver will be required, possibly as many as 50 pieces per guest. All such items have to be delivered to table in the right order and at the right time. (Something I must emphasise here is that all items of silverware should be checked after the meal. One can never be too trusting of the staff and you will be at liberty to take the cost of any missing items, and for that matter any broken items, out of their wages.)

Dining Out

If you are fortunate enough to be dining in a restaurant then the same formalities and observances should apply as we have outlined previously. One must be aware of the rules for both gentlemen and ladies, and observe them. The latter should remember that, while it is acceptable for an unmarried lady to dine out, she must be chaperoned. Lunch or breakfast may be taken alone if the restaurant is deemed respectable; however, it is better for two ladies to dine together if at all possible.

If, as a lady, you are arranging a restaurant dinner, then your guests should assemble at your house so that you can all arrive at the restaurant together. An unmarried gentleman may meet his guests at the restaurant; it is not acceptable for an unmarried lady to arrive alone at the restaurant.

If Charles has business in London we sometimes travel together and experience the grander restaurants, occasionally even the Ritz or Savoy, where we have enjoyed the cooking of Auguste Escoffier, the highly respected French chef. The Savoy continues to maintain the English tradition and requests all diners to be appropriately attired. Ladies are

Not everyone can afford dinner parties.

required to wear dinner gowns but may remove their hats, and gentlemen are still expected to wear a dress suit. If you are not appropriately dressed you may well be asked to leave (as were an earl and his countess recently).

For those who do not live in London and cannot visit Claridge's or the Savoy we have in Bradford both the Midland and the Victoria hotels for formal dining. If you require lunch or simply a cup of tea or coffee then you can do no better than a visit to Collinson's Cafe on Tyrrel Street where a variety of teas and coffees are served, sometimes accompanied by a small orchestra.

If you are dining out or giving a dinner party at home you would be wise to heed the guidance I have given, but if you are simply having a family meal then all these rules become a little laborious and are not strictly necessary. For example, some people are not partial to soup and choose to leave this course out; you may well decide to pass your plate to the head of the table to have meat placed upon it, but please remember that these changes may only take place behind closed doors; once you are under public scrutiny again then a return to the details that I have discussed is wise if you are to avoid humiliation.

In all situations, the rules of dining etiquette must not be allowed to get in the way of a lively table. Polite and entertaining conversation is at all times required. The table must be a happy place where past disagreements are left behind, particularly for family occasions.

An 11-year-old Noel Coward in his acting debut, 1910.

Health

The Edwardian period was a time of lotions, potions and cure-alls; the papers were full of remedies for every imaginable illness and disease, obesity then being classed as a disease.

Advice came both from companies, who were simply promoting their own products, and doctors attending the Royal Family. Some of these remedies are now considered utterly dangerous – such as the recommendation for Belladonna drops in the eyes to dilate the pupils.

Competitors in the first ever *Daily Mirror* glamour competition, 1909.

As an avid reader of the newspapers and journals, I have collected many ideas for cures and guidance on how to cope with illness and disease.

Regrettably, our country still suffers from diseases such as diphtheria and tuberculosis, which can be dealt with only by a physician. The poorer members of our society still struggle to secure medical help and I am aware that it is the high cost of this that prevents many from receiving the assistance they need and deserve. A visit from the doctor together with any medicines prescribed can be an expensive outlay for any family.

Whatever the family situation, all households should try to maintain a basic supply of everyday medicines and keep them out of reach of the children yet in a place where they can be found easily and quickly. I would suggest the following essential items be kept at all times:

Castor oil: *to help digestion, avoid constipation and to stave off colds.*

Camphorated oil: *to ease coughs and chest complaints (this should be rubbed into the chest or even in the children's clothing).*

Eucalyptus oil: *to ease muscle and joint pains, also as a decongestant to help with coughs. It may also be used to help kill any bacteria in the room where a person has been sick.*

Inhaler: *to ease coughs and blocked noses or any general breathing difficulties. If finances permit, I suggest a Wright's Coal Tar Vaporiser.*

If constipation is rife then a laxative will be in order. Cures do not necessarily need to be obtained from a chemist. Naturally occurring items such as prunes, rhubarb, and senna should be sufficient; castor oil can also be used. If you choose to use a chemist then you may find a product such as Gregory's Powder useful. This is a mixture of rhubarb, ginger and magnesia; alternatively, brimstone (sulphur) mixed with treacle may suffice. This is a cure I particularly recommend.

When lack of sleep becomes a problem the use of chloral may be of assistance. This is a mixture of chlorine and alcohol.

Above all, a good diet can aid everyone in keeping poor health at bay. When the weather is cold a substantial meal of fatty meat, hot soups, suet puddings and a cup of hot milk before bed will go a long way to preserving you and your family in good health.

How to Alleviate a Cold

There are many cures for a cold, most of them very simple to prepare. A simple mixture of hot lemonade made with fresh lemon juice and boiling water, sweetened with honey, is one I use when my own family begin to suffer; honey taken on its own will help relieve a sore throat and cough. When retiring for the night a little eucalyptus oil soaked into an old handkerchief and laid on a bedside table may help. Inhaling the fumes whilst asleep will greatly relieve any breathing difficulties.

Those who feel the cold may warm their feet before going to bed by having two basins of water prepared, one fairly cold and the other as hot as can be borne. First, both feet should be placed in the hot water and then plunged into the cold. Once the process has been repeated several times the feet can be dried and you can slip on some bed socks. A hot water bottle may be added to complete the cure.

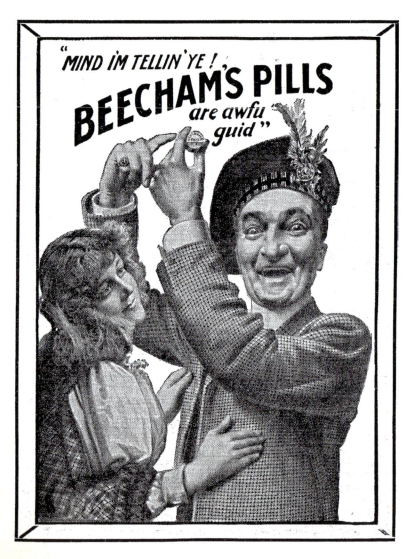

Toothache and Neuralgia

Toothache can occur at any time and is particularly distressing at night time when a visit to the dentist is impossible. A hot water bottle laid against the area may well soothe the pain and allow you to sleep; and in many cases the pain will have gone or at least reduced by the time you wake up. Neuralgia or nerve pains may be soothed by the application of a bag filled with hot salt or bran, since this retains the heat much longer than a hot water bottle.

Earache and Chilblains

Children are particularly susceptible to earache and may have a little warm salad oil dropped into the ear. Be absolutely sure that the oil is only just warm, or it will cause intense pain when placed into the ear. It is best to have the child rest their head, on a pillow for example, so that the afflicted ear is facing uppermost. The child should remain in this position for a few minutes to allow the oil to settle.

When chilblains are noticed an application of turpentine should be used. Try to keep the hands and feet warm without holding them close to the fire. Wear mittens to keep the hands warm and lightweight woollen stockings for the feet.

An Attack of Croup

A baby attacked by croup is of utmost concern to any mother or nurse. A doctor should be sent for immediately but in the meantime you can soak some flannels in very hot water and place them on the child's throat. Change them often so as to keep up the flow of steam. A croupy cough may also be eased with the use of a liberal rubbing of turpentine over the

Exercise for some ladies. A golf match, 1907.

body (this must be used externally only). A covering of Vaseline must then be used to prevent the turpentine from burning. In the absence of Vaseline lard can be used.

Teeth and Gum Diseases

Many children suffer from poor teeth and gums; this can be due to poor diet and also to the type of food given them. These are problems that are not necessarily confined to poor families – they are something all of us have to bear in mind.

One leading doctor suggests we give our children chop bones to gnaw on for the first two years. He believes that chewing is most important and some of the foods we give our children do not require enough chewing. He says: *"this pernicious habit of feeding the young human on pap, is responsible for the horrible condition of the teeth of the inhabitants of these islands"* – strong words indeed, but advice we as parents must be conscious of and act upon.

I cannot highlight sufficiently that a child needs to chew in order to alleviate the dental problems which befall so many of our children and lead to severe problems in later life. The good doctor finishes his comments with this final observation:

"When I think of the millions of unsightly jaws containing irregular teeth, decaying teeth, dead teeth, of the multitude of young men and women wearing artificial dentures, urgent reform becomes the more insistent."

General Medical Tips

Many mothers will have experienced the difficulties of getting their child to take a medicine with a disagreeable taste. The most common of these is likely to be a dose of castor oil. The objections may be overcome by taking a wine glass and rubbing a lemon around the rim, putting in the necessary dose and then squeezing a little more lemon juice into the glass. This should be accepted quite easily. An orange is of equal benefit.

In the case of wounds such as a splinter or nail or possibly a cut from a knife, wash the wound with turpentine and warm water. This will burn for a few moments but acts as an antiseptic and a small wound should heal itself very soon.

A Healthy Diet

Children must receive a variety of foods, including sugar and starch. Starch should be given by means such as a well-baked crust of bread spread with butter, dripping or bacon fat. A hard biscuit will suffice but it is less nutritious than the former.

Sugar must be kept to meagre proportions until the third or possibly fourth year. Sugar cane may be regarded differently, and can be chewed on since the sugar content is diluted and the chewing exercises the jaw in a most efficient manner. Once the baby's first teeth are cut then the introduction of some hard fruit or perhaps a leathery crust of bread can be advised.

Many are the days when, as a mother or wife, you feel lethargic and worn out; you may have aches and pains and even feel depressed. On such occasions work is out of the question, friends may bore, the children become a nuisance. Life itself becomes dark and dreary. Such days are common – but not unavoidable. When a woman is in this state of depression and hopelessness and misery it is a sign she has fallen victim to one of the many ailments and disorders to which a woman's constitution is particularly prone.

Children play in a Bradford street.

The more observant of you may well recognise these words are not entirely my own, and you would be correct. I quote from the newspaper advertisement for Bile Beans. I cannot recommend this product highly enough.

Bile Beans are recommended not just for women. The whole family may benefit from their use, because they offer a cure for so many illnesses – headaches, constipation, piles, liver chill, bad breath, influenza, flatulence, rheumatism, indigestion, palpitations, sleeplessness, anaemia, dizziness and many, many more. They have been scientifically tested as well, so you may be assured of their efficacy. In fact you will read many testimonials as to their value: I include one here, by way of illustration:

Dark Days Brightened.

Bile Beans banished the dark days of my suffering. I had indigestion and aches and pains all the time, so much so I was constantly depressed. In fact it got so bad that I thought many times of doing away with myself!
One night I was in such agony I thought I were on the eve of my death!
I could hardly move and lay wasting in my bed for many days. Two doctors attended me but neither was able to offer me relief from my pains. At last a neighbour persuaded me to try Bile Beans and in a short time my strength was restored. Within a very short time I was back to strength and able to take up the housework again ! I have been well for some time now and I believe this cure is a permanent one.

Another food I wish to draw to your attention is grape nuts, a highly nutritious and health-giving item that all families should have in their kitchens. Those who have trouble taking ordinary foods when ill may find grape nuts are perfectly palatable.

My own mother suffered for many years with liver and lung disease. This led to a loss of appetite, and her health deteriorated at an alarming rate, so much so that our family physician asked my father to "prepare for the worst"; at the time she was only taking a little milk and was nearly starved. It was suggested to father that he try a packet of grape nuts.

We had all read about them but had never tried them. The change was astonishing. Mother would quite often manage three bowls a day, and her health improved week after week until she was able to eat normal food again. A quite remarkable recovery was witnessed in our very own family – and so I am able to recommend them to you with complete assurance.

I have been fascinated recently with a discovery that one's finger nails can be a sign of one's immediate health and even indicate as yet unseen problems. The nail of a healthy person grows about one-sixteenth of an inch each week, but during illness or following an accident or any mental depression the growth (both in length and in thickness) is retarded; thus the very slightest illness will leave an indelible mark on the nails, which may be readily detected. For example, if one has a sudden attack of acute rheumatism and the body temperature is sent bounding upwards, within a space of two or three hours the effect can be seen in the nails. If the illness is slower, as with typhoid fever, then the nails will show poor growth and thickness.

"The SECRET of my good health has been Bovril!"

BOVRIL

repels colds, chills and influenza

Obesity

Obesity has long been a humiliating and debilitating condition that restricts one from living a normal healthy life. Some doctors tell us to simply reduce the amount we eat and to add some exercise to our daily routines. This is not always satisfactory advice, since reducing one's food intake can leave one listless and deprived of the stamina needed to go about one's daily routine. My advice is to try a bottle of Antipon tonic. I have spoken to many people who have been amazed at the results. The dramatic loss of weight is quite remarkable and long-lasting.

If you are of a stout disposition you will sit enviously watching other ladies bathe at resorts. You may have had to give up sports you once enjoyed such as cycling or tennis and the simple act of walking will leave you breathless. The use of this tonic means that food can be taken as normal, without any need for reducing quantities. The purchase of a bottle of Antipon tonic will also be of benefit to men who find their activities curtailed. One gentleman apparently lost 18 pounds in a fortnight. I leave this subject with one remarkable testimonial:

"When I started Antipon I was 246lbs in weight and the reduction since starting with it (Antipon) is 62lbs. I can now take a four mile walk with ease. Besides its reducing qualities another recommendation is its power of reducing gracefully, for my skin is quite tightened and not flaccid in the least. My heart, which is diseased, is stronger and is beating healthier."

The very thin woman, on the other hand, must follow an entirely different regime if she is to put flesh on her bones. If she is inclined to worry she should try to be less intense regarding unimportant matters; she should shut her eyes, in a sense, to everything tiresome. The troubles that never happen wear out the nerves and destroy health more completely than those that do materialise. She should read only pleasant books and talk as much as possible.

Finally, before moving on to the matter of the female complexion, I turn to a rather delicate matter.

Those who have suffered from ruptures will know this is an extremely painful condition to live with, and requires the utmost care and attention. Like obesity, a rupture can severely restrict enjoyment of certain activities that you previously enjoyed. You may well have taken to wearing a truss,

No more Drunkenness.

which will keep the rupture (or hernia, to give it its proper name) from tearing any further. There are many advertisements in the newspapers for devices that will help you to carry on with as normal a life as possible. Taking time off work to have an operation may be out of the question for some and there is always a danger associated with any medical procedure. Messrs W M Rice Ltd can offer a cure without the need for a perilous operation, and I quote from their advertisement.

Women's Well-being

In the Edwardian era, advertising specifically targeted women. This was true not just for medicines but also for the emerging cosmetics market. Women were seen as weak and prone to emotional outpourings, and it was thought they needed time to calm themselves, primarily so they could attend to matters of the house and looking after their hard-working husbands. The papers were full of new, exciting and marvellous remedies that would restore their vigour, vitality and their looks.

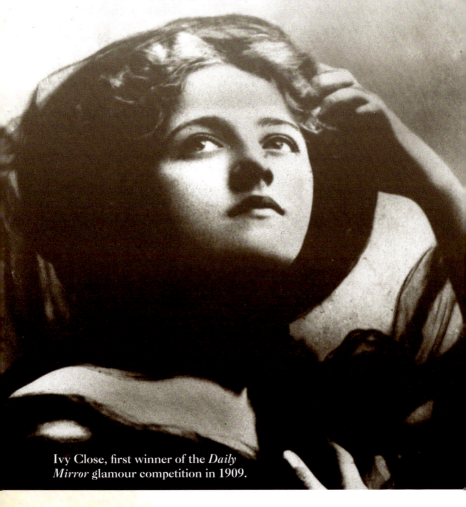

Ivy Close, first winner of the *Daily Mirror* glamour competition in 1909.

As wives, mothers or single ladies, we constantly strive to look our best at all times, realising we are judged according to how we dress, how we conduct ourselves and, perhaps most stringently, how we look.

I have therefore brought together information that will help you attain the standards that are expected of us. Since we are also forever battling against the signs of ageing, I offer advice from some older women who have managed to keep time at bay. If the advance of age cannot be reduced its effects can certainly be alleviated.

Let me start with the complexion. While we have to accept what God has given us in terms of beauty, many aspects of our appearance can be attributed to how we live. For example, women of a high colour are probably large eaters and shy away from any exercise that may tire them. Eating is the prime area we need to look at. A diet of rich food does not help one's complexion or figure, and must be reduced. A pale skin, on the other hand, is associated with those who spend little time outdoors; and a skin that is too pale may be a sign of illness, so precautions should be taken. Yet those with an olive skin should not be regarded as sickly; there may simply be some foreign ancestor to account for their colour. A purple complexion is usually a sign of some problem with the heart.

Car owners gather for an outing, c.1904.

It is essential that a woman takes great care when washing her face. The aim in all cases is to keep the pores of the face open so they can perform their function adequately. If you suffer from any eruption on the face, I advise the use of warm water. This will speed up the flow of blood and help to clear the area. You should also avoid cold water when the weather is warm or when you have a hot face – in fact it is wise to apply the simple rule of warm water in summer and cold water in winter, following the pattern of temperatures outside. One should always use a pure soap and rinse thoroughly, then apply a light powder and let it dry. It is best to take soft linen, rather than coarse towels, to dry the face – remember that our skin is delicate, much the same as porcelain. I would also recommend the use of a good cold cream, possibly one made from wool fat and cucumber juices. This is easily absorbed into the skin and doesn't leave a greasy film.

Sunburn can cause enormous damage to our skin, and so special care must be taken to avoid any permanent disfigurement. Particular caution must be exercised when a visit to the coast has been undertaken. A combination of sun and wind can cause untold havoc. You must also be aware that some of the clothes now in fashion such as fine lace blouses and muslins allow the sun to penetrate to the skin, and so when you come to wear an evening gown you will find the neck and throat a most unseemly colour.

An inexpensive cure for sunburn and the effects of the outdoors is to steam the face and use a good cold cream.

The Eyes

"What the sun is to the earth, the eyes are to the human face, not only a crowning glory, but the source of all light ." Anon

It is so easy to neglect this area where the utmost attention is required. If you have

been out walking – or, for those lucky enough, enjoyed a motor car journey – your eyes will be full of dust and possibly rather red. An accumulation of dust not only makes the eyelids swell but also prevents the eyelashes from growing. To prevent this condition the eyes must be bathed regularly in an eye-bath, preferably using a lotion similar to the following preparation:

Boric acid......20 grains
Compound tincture of lavender......20 drops
Rose water sufficient to make 4 ounces

Mix into a lotion and bathe the eyes.

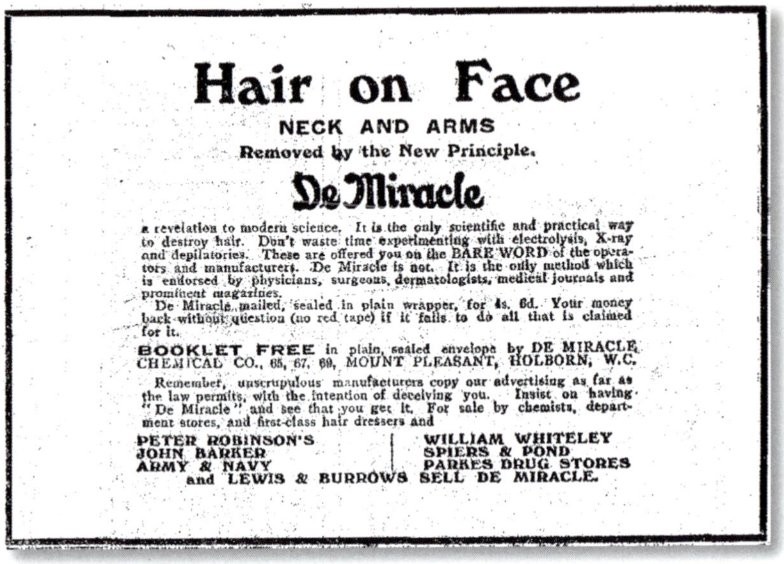

Never rub the eyes, because this causes inflammation. You may use a preparation of the juice of a strawberry strained through a piece of linen or try elderberry water for painful or itching eyes. Always give your eyes a rest and never read or sew in a weak light; gazing at minute objects for too long should also be avoided.

Freckles

Freckles are the bane of many women, particularly blondes and sometimes brunettes with fair skin. The only remedy is to bleach them. Neither cream nor ointment can remove them, since they are formed deep down in the skin. One has to exercise patience in using this treatment because it is a long process to rid yourself of these unsightly blemishes. Apply the lotion with either cotton wool or a camelhair brush (though the latter is preferable in my experience).

Freckle Bleaching Lotion

Peroxide Hydrogen (10% volume)......1 ounce

Eau de Cologne......1 ounce

Glycerine and rose water......1 ounce

Depilatories

A growth of hair on the upper lip or chin is unsightly and gives a somewhat masculine appearance. The only really effective solution is to use a pair of steel tweezers and remove each hair individually; and the hairs must be carefully pulled and not broken. Recently an operation called "electrolysis", involving the use of electricity, has been available, but it rarely works and is always painful.

Care of the Hands

It is advisable to adopt a routine of care for your hands every night before retiring. Even if you do not use them for housework or gardening, merely exposing them to the air can cause damage. Yet do not fear! Using only a few simple items will enable you to maintain hands that look and feel beautiful. These are: a nail brush, a box of rose paste, nail powder, a vial of ammonia, almond meal and a lemon.

The pumice stone is used to smooth down calloused hands, while stains may be removed by using lemon juice, borax or ammonia. Especial attention must be paid to the nails: they should be cut to the shape of the end of the finger and the surface should be polished. One hour a week should be sufficient.

Those who have limited means should not forget that the kitchen can supply many of the necessary ingredients for a good complexion. Milk can be used to bathe the face, and the addition of a spoonful of sulphur to a cup of milk can help with any discoloration. A handful

of oatmeal gently rubbed over the skin whilst washing will help create a smooth, refined skin.

Whilst you are taking every care of your skin you may be aggrieved that there are other conditions one cannot apparently halt.

Insect bites, for instance, are the scourge of the outdoor life and can put an end to a jolly and spirited day out. A garden party or simply a picnic can be ruined by the midge. Wearing a veil or long gloves is the usual approach, but it is hard to sit swathed in such garments whilst the sun beats down. What is needed is a preparation that will repel these obnoxious creatures and yet is harmless to use. The preparation must be rubbed on arms, face and throat *before* going out into the sun. If open-work stockings are worn then a little rubbed on the ankles and legs will help. I find this lotion excellent for keeping away not only the midge but also mosquitoes, gnats and the particularly detestable harvest bug. This horrid little creature enjoys the "happy hunting ground" of the corn field and seems particularly attracted to my ankles.

Oil of lavender......10 drops
Oil of eucalyptus......1 ½ drachms (⅛ fluid ounce)
Spirits of camphor......1 ounce
Soap liniment......1 ½ ounces

Apply as directed.

The term to "grow old gracefully" may be rather easier to say than to accomplish, but I would like to include a piece of advice that my mother often quoted when discussing the matter.

"Go to bed early and arise early" will help you keep your youthful looks. Late nights and oversleeping are ruinous to the complexion. If, however, late nights are impossible to avoid then take an afternoon nap – even one hour will suffice. Before retiring for the night take a warm bath, without remaining in the water for long. Then drink a cup of bouillon and a small glass of Malaga wine. Rise no earlier than 10 o'clock and take a cold plunge or sponge bath followed by a light breakfast. A daily walk is essential, though, again, do not remain outside for too long as the sun will start to damage the complexion.

In some circles the use of scents, rouge and face powders are not approved of, being considered too "common"; in such situations natural beauty is the aspiration. A simple rose water or lavender certainly satisfies my own needs, but I am sure some of you will wish to know what else may be obtained.

Many of the fragrances popular today are based on such plants as bergamot, lavender, mint or sweet marjoram, and are usually described as fern fragrances. The most notable is that created by the house of Guerlain, called Après L'Ondée. Guerlain have a rival in François Coty, who presents his perfumes in ornate, purpose-made bottles. Coty opened a shop next door to René Lalique, the great Art Nouveau jeweller, glassmaker and designer, on the Place Vendôme in Paris. Lalique has produced some of the most exquisite bottles; and I am proud to have two or three in my possession.

It is said that Queen Alexandra has retained her youthful looks by the use of "enamel" on the face. This gives a pale white appearance, which is the favoured complexion today, but is not considered safe by some. Another procedure that some see as unsafe is the use of belladonna drops in the eye to dilate the pupil.

For those wishing to "paint the face", enamel is the first layer to be applied. It is made of white lead in a cream base. The next step is to apply a rice or pearl powder, to give a smooth appearance to the skin. (Some of you may well know already

of *papier poudre*, the powder that comes in books of coloured paper and helps to remove unwanted shine from cheeks and noses.) Rouge and lip-rouge may follow next. I have heard that some women have their lips and cheeks tattooed so they stay permanently coloured. Eyebrows are highlighted with an eyebrow pencil and very occasionally some women will use a drop of belladonna to make the pupils enlarge. Most doctors claim this to be a dangerous practice.

Shopping for cosmetics is seen by many as something to be done in privacy, with women visiting stores heavily veiled and some shops having their entrances in a side street. But since Gordon Selfridge has opened his store in London women are becoming more used to seeing cosmetics right on the front counter and are encouraged to choose and experiment. I visited on one occasion but found it difficult to avail myself of this new method, but many shops and stores are now following this innovation and it has become usual for women to shop in the open, as it were.

The common term for make-up is "painting the face", which is still seen by some as something only actors and actresses should do. Here is a warning to women about how to approach this "art".

"The best advice to those contemplating painting their face is that there is a thoroughly right and wrong way of doing it. In this matter the art of concealing is of primary importance. Ladies who powder and paint in supposed imitation of the heightened charms of singers and actresses are apt to forget that these latter are only seen at a distance, which adds a charm to the broad and glaring effect, precisely as it does to the coarse daubing of the scene painter."

Children

Children were still to be "seen and not heard" in this period. They were kept separated from their parents, occasionally joining them for meals and family entertainment. For the better off, many of the toys familiar today were available, from dolls and toy soldiers to bicycles and, for the fortunate, the first easy-to-use cameras. Children of the working classes, however, were often sent out to work in order to support the family, and so received minimal education.

Yet changes were afoot, in clothing as in other fields. Baby boys were ceasing to wear dresses and girls were wearing less restrictive outfits. The "sailor suit" arrived as the standard outfit for the young child.

Actress Miss Kathleen Severn on stage, 1906.

I would like to recommend Miss Ada Ballin's *From Cradle to School*, published by Constable, as an aid to child care.

"No household is complete without children, or at any rate one little toddler, or baby lying asleep in its cot, but ruling the household with an autocratic if unconscious sway."

Having two children of my own, and twins at that, has seen our household dominated for many years by children and their needs. We have been fortunate in having the means to look after them properly and school them well. Between my husband and I we have taught them respect and manners, and they are growing up to be worthy adults.

Yet each day going to and from my shop, I see children who are less fortunate, children who are playing in the street in what amounts to rags, many with no shoes on their feet. Their schooling has been extremely limited and many have parents who struggle to keep them fed, let alone well clothed and educated. I am told that many of our poorer children are dying simply from a lack of suitable, warm clothing.

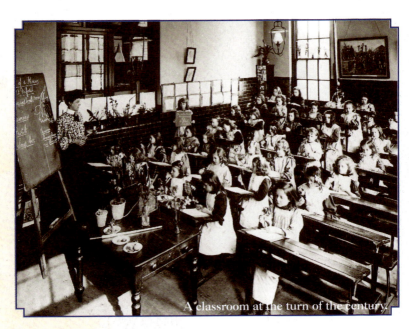

A classroom at the turn of the century.

Lady Elizabeth Bowes-Lyon and her brother David, 1909.

Too many children in a family is a source of problems for the poorer members of our society. Recently I was told about a family in the city with 10 children, and the father unable to work through injury. The mother took in some washing and worked as a cleaner in a number of houses. To judge by the children's ages she must have had one child a year.

We are still prone to many serious diseases, such as tuberculosis and diphtheria, both of which contribute to the high mortality rate amongst our infants. Bereavement, for the poorer child, is all too common. There cannot be many who have not experienced either a sibling, parent or even a friend dying.

Some of you may well have seen the play *Peter Pan* by J M Barrie. As Peter faced possible death by drowning he is heard to say *"to die will*

be an *awfully big adventure*". It has been suggested that this line was deliberately introduced by Barrie to help children with their understanding of death. If so, Barrie may have been speaking from experience: his own brother died aged 13.

There are now so many aids available for bringing up a child. I am sure many of you will be familiar with the products of Allenbury's. Not only do they offer a bottle for feeding but a range of foods to help the baby grow. Of course normal adult food should

be avoided until the child is at least 8 to 10 months old; their digestion cannot cope with the solid food we eat. You may have heard about the present debate regarding whether feeding a baby cow's milk or using one of these proprietary foods is better. Some doctors say that these new foods are causing harm since they are not "natural", like the milk of a cow. I have brought my own children up on these new foods and found no harm whatsoever in them, in fact quite the opposite.

Allenbury's products are possibly the best known and the ones I can recommend from personal experience. They offer three types of baby food for the first few weeks of life, then another for the seventh or eighth month and finally a malted food which should bring the baby up to the start of solid foods, nearer to adult fare. They have also introduced the "rusk". This is a type of crisp biscuit, similar to toast, specially made from a selection of flours to aid muscle growth. It has particular benefits in helping the first teeth to come through, through the action of chewing. You may also purchase from Allenbury's a food that is suitable for ailing adults who need to regain their strength.

Working class children gather in the street.

Useful additions to a baby's nursery are teething pegs. These strips of ivory allow the baby to chew and so to ease the suffering from sore gums and the arrival of their first teeth. You will find that each set of pegs has a different shape to allow baby to explore with both their mouth and their fingers, thus keeping them amused for some time and, it must be said, quiet.

Books are of prime importance to your child's education, and a suitable selection should be available at all times. I have already mentioned Mr J M Barrie's *Peter Pan* but there are a multitude of others. Beatrix Potter's *Peter Rabbit*, suitable for the very young, is not only a delightful story but beautifully illustrated too. Rudyard Kipling's *Just So* stories are for the slightly older child. My son adores *How the Leopard got his Spots*, which

has been read many times in our house. Another favourite of the whole family is Kenneth Grahame's *Wind in the Willows*, the tale of Rat, Mole and Badger – such a delight. My daughter Emily's favourite is a recent publication, *The Secret Garden* by Frances Hodgson Burnett, describing how Frances really discovered a secret garden when she lived at Great Maytham Hall in Kent. Finally, a long-time favourite, *Alice's Adventures in Wonderland* by Lewis Carroll; once again there are beautiful illustrations to complement a fine story.

Toys and games are naturally very important to the child. Even where families cannot provide anything more stimulating than an old doll

and possibly some wooden blocks, still children will play with them and love them.

The toy bear is probably the most popular toy amongst the younger children – or perhaps I should refer to it by the new name of the "teddy bear". This wonderful name came from America, where it is said that the owner of the company who produced the bears saw a cartoon of President Edward ("Teddy")Roosevelt refusing to shoot a bear cub and hence the "teddy bear" was born.

If you have a boy in the family you may find they like a new toy called Meccano. Using miniature nuts and bolts, metal plates and bases, they can build all sorts of structures and designs. Edward adores Meccano (as does his father, when time permits). Yet this activity is of no interest to girls; neither Emily nor myself can see the fun to be had in something quite so "industrial". Emily much prefers her collection of dolls, some of which were my own and one very special one with a porcelain head, belonging to her grandmother. Board games are plentiful in the house and our favourite is Minoru, a horse racing game named after King Edward's racehorse, which won the Derby for him in 1909. Charles and I have one slight reservation about this game in that it encourages gambling, as if one were at a real race meeting, and is possibly not the most educational; however, it is only a game.

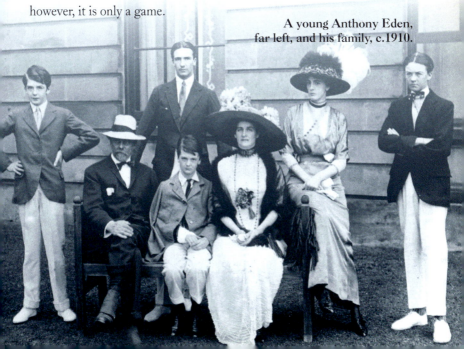

A young Anthony Eden, far left, and his family, c.1910.

Some children may be lucky enough to own a personal camera, but for many this is simply a dream. The "Box Brownie" allows much easier taking of photographs than the normal and very large plate cameras. These were cumbersome, and when one had taken the pictures you had to develop them yourself, which involved some potentially unpleasant chemicals. I was never too keen on having one of these in the house, despite many pleas from Edward.

"The absence of discipline and control in early life are the natural foundations of failure later on – failure through the lack of control which underlies all weakness of character, vice and criminality." – Dr Truby King

One may think this too harsh a judgement, but children need control and they need guidelines. It is all too easy for them to take the wrong path and come into conflict with the forces of law and order. Disobedience and defiance of authority is not to be tolerated at any time. Punishment may take several forms. The use of the "strap" may be enough to reproach some children or even the use of the hand in some cases. The withdrawal of privileges is the method I try to use more often. You may also instigate some menial tasks for the child to complete or isolate them by returning them to their room.

Boys, in particular, need good discipline, and it is with this in mind that I suggest you find a local meeting of the newly formed Scouting movement. If your son is between the ages of

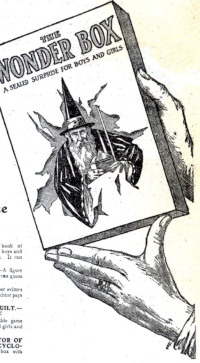

12 and 16 he can join one of these groups. The Founder of the movement, Sir Robert Baden-Powell, discovered, during his time as a military leader during the Boer War, that many potential new recruits had to be refused because they were unfit and lacked moral fibre; this was especially true of our working-class youth.

The Scout movement aims to teach boys to be independent and

confident. The boys learn to be practical by means of outdoor activities such as camping and hiking; and in time it is hoped they will become useful and helpful citizens. I have read that even some girls wish to join to this group and that Sir Robert's sister, Agnes, has set up an organisation for them too (the Girl Guides Association, I believe). But of course girls will also be taught the necessary needlecraft and domestic needs at home or through school.

"A minimum of 40 buttons on my underwear alone, a liberty bodice like a coat of mail, and starched lace of my chemise that prickled like a ring of thorns around my neck. It could be a good hour's hard-work to get dressed in a morning." – Anon

I am sure many of you will recognise this description and share the sentiments expressed. Not all families of course are able to afford to clothe

Family outing to the beach, 1901.

their children with an array of outfits to suit all occasions. The poorer family may need to pass down clothes from the older child to the younger and keep them in as good condition as possible; the mother with good sewing skills uses patterns that are to be found in newspapers and journals and makes the clothes herself; usually it is a matter of repairing each garment as necessary. If you are fortunate to afford new clothes then there are new materials and designs to satisfy everyone.

The materials used these days are far lighter in weight than we have been used to – the heavy flannels and dark colours, the legacy of our dear Queen and her mourning requirements. Nowadays soft fabrics such as silk and muslin are readily available. We older girls can acceptably wear pastel colours, pale creams and ivory, and their garments decorated with fancy embroidery and sashes of lemon and mauve – unheard of when I was a child. However, for the younger child it is best to keep to white for the entire wardrobe.

Dresses will come below the knee for the very young girl, but may be above the knee when older; I have observed in the last few years that short sleeves are becoming popular as well; when outdoors a straw boater may be worn to complement the outfit.

For the boy the choice of clothing is much simpler. In the early years

A day with family and friends, c.1910.

a "sailor suit" is most satisfactory. This will comprise of a hat or cap, blouse and short pants (until the child is a little older, when he may wear long pants). This suit is a miniature of the uniform worn by sailors in the British Navy and is a delight to observe. You may even add a lanyard with a small brass whistle to finish off the outfit.

It is wise to discourage your children from mixing and playing with those of a lesser class. Bad influences are picked up all too easily and may undo the good work you have striven for with your own children. With adults as with children: good manners must be observed at all times. Children should not ask about what another's father does for a living, for example, or how much they earn. When they are with you at table they must observe the same social graces and etiquette as adults. (Our son Edward has a habit of placing his elbows on the table, causing Charles to get most upset. He is often to be heard quoting from his mother who used to say, "*All joints on the table will be carved!*". This usually persuades Edward to remove his elbows immediately.)

Fashion

The female fashion of this period can be summed up as big hats, long dresses and corsets. A woman could take over an hour to put on the array of petticoats, blouses and skirts that were required and, as is always the case, if you didn't have means to dress in this way you had to "make do and mend".

"An Edwardian lady in full dress was a wonder to behold, and her preparations for viewing were awesome." – William Manchester, American Historian

As I run my own dressmaking and millinery business it is incumbent upon me to keep up with the current fashions. So much has started to change in what we women wear and how we wear it since our beloved Queen Victoria died that we have been able to lighten our dress and take on some

You could even have a dress designed specifically to play bridge in.

A typical Edwardian bathing outfit.

of the more interesting designs from Paris and around the world.

Since King Edward has been on the throne there has been a new burst of interest in what we wear. He has brought back influences from his travels around the globe (although I am none too sure of his fancy to wear a black tie with a dinner suit).

Wealth is still the divider between good dress and poor. I notice that my girls in the shop, whilst I pay them as well as can be expected, wear the same dress and blouse day after day. Some of them have only two outfits in all.

Many of my clients wish to purchase the latest fashions but are not in a position to visit the couture houses in London or even, for that matter, the larger department stores such as Harrods; that is why they come to me and ask me to make copies. The newspapers regularly show the new designs, and so, with a little skill and application, my girls can usually replicate a design that closely resembles the original at a more affordable price.

The girls I employ are all good, hard workers and I am conscious that they work long hours to create beautiful dresses which they could never afford themselves. But they take pride in what they do and are content to see a satisfied client.

There are so many influences on ladies' fashion today that it is hard to keep up. The slim silhouette we have been encouraged to display can be achieved only with the corset. Whilst this has been a necessary evil for some women, designs are changing and the new, freer designs we are beginning to see are kinder to our health in many ways.

Hair

The way we dress our hair not only forms a major part of the new look, it also tells us much about the wearer, as if the hair were a symbol of the whole person. When a lady reaches maturity, wearing her hair up may be interpreted as a sign that she is ready for marriage – that she has grown up and must no longer be seen or treated as a girl. On the other hand, it has been said in some circles that loose undressed hair is a sign of virginity (although I have heard it said that it also signifies a promiscuous woman, which is all very confusing).

Edwardian bridal gown. 1910.

To dress the hair is a long and arduous task, for which the maid usually provides assistance. She can wrap the hair round and round, padding it to give it the "full" look. A task you may prefer to reserve to yourself is saving any hair that has been brushed out or which has fallen to the floor, and then working it back into the hair to add body.

Looking after the hair adequately is an important part of a lady's routine, and so here I offer some tips that you may find useful. I recall this first one from a newspaper article written to Mrs Templer, the regular columnist offering advice to women. The advice is always given from the viewpoint of a girl, Cecily, talking to Mrs Templer:

"How often should hair be washed ?" asked Cecily.

"Not more than once a month," said Mrs Templer.

"And what about hair dyes, is there not a cosmetic that some people rub on their hair to hide grey tresses ?"

"Yes," answered Mrs Templer; "many women like to rub a cosmetic prepared by melting some nicely scented soap powder and adding either lamp-black or

umber ground in almond oil.
These colours can be bought
ready ground in any artists'
colourman and should be added
when the soap is soft."

I love reading the advice Mrs
Templer used to give. Here is
another of her tips:

The 'NEENA' (TRADE MARK) Bust Protector & Improver

Modelled from the VENUS DE MILO.

OF ALL DRAPERS AND LADIES' OUTFITTERS.
LARGE OR SMALL SIZE, 4/11;
POST FREE, 5/-. FOR EVENING, 7/6 per pair.

The 'NEENA' imparts an exquisite grace and beauty to the figure and protects the bust. Held in position by any close-fitting garment.

The "NEENA" is perfectly effective, light, and hygienic, its presence cannot be detected, and thin figures should take advantage of the invention.—"THE QUEEN." and most satisfactory device, and few can dispense with the wonderful improvement the A novel and most satisfactory device, and few can dispense with the wonderful improvement the "Neena" effects in the figure.—"THE TATLER." and will be welcomed by all ladies. A special shape, The "Neena" leaves nothing to be desired, and will be welcomed by all ladies. A special shape, daintily trimmed with fine Valenciennes lace, can be recommended for evening wear.—"LADY'S PIC. TORIAL." Girls who indulge in hockey, tennis, or fencing will find that the "Neena" Bust Protector renders blows (always possible events) quite harmless, and gives to the figure an elegant and natural effect.— "THE LADY." Manufacturers: The 'NEENA' CO., Ltd.. 88/90, Chancery Lane, LONDON, W.C.

The Cult of Comliness

"And now could you tell me
how to wash my hair?" asked Cecily. "I have been using lemon juice and this has
made the hair too dry."

"I do not believe in the use of lemon juice at all, unless it is amalgamated with
some form of oil," said Mrs Templer.

The newspapers are always full of tonics and lotions that promise to keep
hair looking at its finest. Charles will not approve of my telling you, but
he has suffered a little thinning around the top of his head and swears by
Edward Harlene's Hair Food.

I quote from one of their adverts:

Are you out of fashion?

The right and the wrong way of cultivating your hair.

*World's greatest hair specialist warns readers of the many unseen dangers
which threaten their hair and shows how, by a simple home method, they can
banish baldness and greyness and vastly enhance the beauty and luxuriance of
their hair.*

*A large trial bottle of his famous hair food and hair tonic, of exactly the same
quality as supplied to his Royal and aristocratic clients.*

*Harlene's hair drill takes up only two or three minutes a day. The hair will
grow back thick and luxuriant!*

The ideal hair colour is considered to be brown, nut-brown or possibly chestnut. Blonde is not a good colour and it is an unfortunate woman who has this colouring.

Hats

Once the hair is arranged a hat is a necessary adornment. My ladies all wear the most fashionable hats and bring me pictures they have seen in the newspapers showing the latest creations. Naturally I travel to shows and purchase some of these creations directly for my wealthier clients, but many ask me to recreate the original. Cost is always an issue and not all ladies living in this part of the country are as wealthy as our London counterparts.

Some of these hats can be topped off with ostrich or even osprey feathers. One then needs the ability to hold such hats on the head – which is no mean feat. For this purpose we sell a range of hat-pins. At first glance they are rather vicious looking, but most necessary; many of them are also very ornate in design.

Undergarments

If I have gone a little ahead of myself I shall now return to that most important feature of ladies dress, the undergarment. Whilst not a topic for general conversation I feel sure that some guidance would be welcome in this area.

As we tried to shake off our Victorian past and enter into this "new world" of fashion, attitudes were also changing as to the purpose of these garments. Our undergarments are no longer simply items of comfort and practicality; they now have another purpose, which is to appeal to men.

There is a new buzz of excitement in this area of dress, with new fabrics – chiffon and taffeta for example – that veritably make ladies "whisper" as they walk by. Brightly coloured undergarments (or may I use the new word, "lingerie") which were once regarded as brash, perhaps best suited to the courtesan rather than the respectable lady, have now, in this new century, become all the mode; at least for those who can afford this kind of luxury. One's lingerie is seen as a status symbol; from where and from whom it was bought can say much about the wearer.

In other respects, too, we Edwardian ladies are "layered", so to speak. Before putting on the essential corset one has to put on "combinations", a sort of vest and pants all in one garment. Occasionally it has short sleeves or shoulder straps, but invariably it goes down to the knees; and the corset is fitted on over the top. The shape women aspire to has changed from Victoria's day: we now strive for an "S" shape. This has a tendency to throw the body forward and allow us to breathe a little more easily, which is a blessing.

One Mme Gashes-Sarraute of Paris has designed a corset that is intended to improve health instead of endangering it. Her aim is to remove pressure from the vital female organs. Yet the demand for a small waist persists, so the maid must be employed in tightening these corsets. A waist of the average 25 to 27 inches can be reduced to one of 20 inches with the right application.

Madame Dowding Corsetière
The Pretty Polly from 15s 6d
A certain cure for obesity and an aid to indigestion which can be reduced
without the slightest inconvenience.
Braces up the figure and gives freedom
of movement to every muscle.

The use of the corset has created much discussion and opinion as to its nature and necessity.

"The corset is, in economic theory substantially a mutilation, undergone for the purpose of lowering the subject's vitality and rendering her permanently and obviously unfit for work." – Thorstein Veblen, Norwegian sociologist

Mr Veblen may be a little draconian in his views, but I tend to agree with him.

After the corset comes the camisole or, as it is sometimes called, a petticoat bodice. Six petticoats are not unusual for the wealthier lady. The cost of these petticoats can be as reasonable as 5s 6d or as much as 50 guineas for the most exquisite lace example.

For the traveller this "sleep suit" was available.

Interestingly, an abundance of undergarments is often regarded as hygienic and to be encouraged.

"Women wore a tremendous amount of underclothes, as compared with today. They wore many petticoats, fringed with lace, which formed an enchanting foam around their ankles." – W McQueen Pope, a contemporary theatre critic

We now come to the knickers, which usually have lace frills at the knee. Occasionally these have buttons at the waist; alternatively they can be taped up; but they are always in white. Stockings are usually made of silk; these can be grey in colour, white or even black. Finally comes the waist-petticoat, again made of silk, tied around the waist.

Naturally, these items of dress apply only to wealthier ladies. Women from the lower classes may possibly try a corset during a holiday period, but other than that their dress is somewhat limited.

Dressed for Ascot, 1900.

The New Look

The height of fashion for the well-dressed lady is a tailored suit. This is a rather masculine look but very practical for women who are moving into work and slightly more active endeavours. I am aware how it came into being – there are many stories about its invention, some fanciful I fear; personally I favour the one that claims Alexandra, Princess of Wales, had a trunk of clothes go missing when she was attending an important dinner and instead of embarrassing the host she asked her maid to cut down her riding habit.

This new style of tailored outfits is seen by some men as a threat to their masculinity. It is true that it reduces the obvious division between how a man should look and how a woman should look. I pointed out to Charles on many occasions that this new trend reflects what women are now able to do; I need to dress comfortably, particularly when at my shop; I need to move freely when going about town and to the functions I attend from time to time. I find this "look" ideal and embrace it wholeheartedly.

The skirts are substantial and full, being fastened tightly at the waist, and then flow out at the bottom, producing a lily like shape. There are disadvantages too, however:

"The discomfort of a walk in the rain in a sodden skirt that wound its wetness round your legs and chapped your ankles…Walking about the London streets trailing clouds of dust was horrid. I once found I had carried into the house a banana skin which had got caught up in the unstitched hem of my dress."

Gloves are an essential element of the lady's outfit. They are usually kid for outdoor and country wear, and silk for the evening. Fur is also popular;

whole animal skins such as fox and mink are draped across the shoulders of some ladies.

One group of people disapproves of wearing animal skins (in fact they seem to object to a lot of things as well). They belong to the "Aesthetic Movement" – indeed, many of them are artists or from an artistic family – and they generally object to the restrictive nature of female attire, particularly items like the bustle and latterly the corset. The movement has its origins in the late Victorian age, but its influence appears now to be spreading in our own times.

They advocate a style of dress for women that is more generously cut and not so tight fitting as the standard fashion of the day dictates. The fabrics they recommend are wool, velvet or Liberty silk. I have always thought they were rather Bohemian in attitude and possibly not to be trusted or relied upon. Many of them have taken to wearing a very white make-up and to dying their hair a reddish colour with the use of henna dye.

These trends aside, once the dress has been decided upon a parasol in summer is necessary, usually of silk and embroidered with fine detail and lace. Handbags are seldom used, other than a very small bag with a fine chain that can be worn around the wrist. One has so little to keep in a bag in any case; purchases can usually be charged to one's account and settled at the end of the month.

Edwardian sportswear, 1908:
ladies' archery competition.

Menswear

One should not neglect male attire, nor even the delicate matter of men's undergarments. For men the first item to consider is the "union suit". This is a full-length, one-piece garment, usually wool with flaps front and back for ease of access.

Until fashions began to follow the trends set by the Prince of Wales, men's attire changed very little over the years. There were perhaps minor changes to the cut of a trouser or a new shape to the jacket, but only relatively recently have styles begun to change significantly. And even here only in certain cases; the working-class man generally possesses only one suit with a shirt and possibly a tie, carefully guarded for special occasions such as weddings or a funeral; he never "dresses" for dinner or attends any society functions.

The gentleman is a different case entirely and has to be properly attired at all times. This requires outfits for the morning, for the evening and for any sporting event he may attend.

Morning dress consists of the morning coat, which is usually a serge material, double-breasted and normally in black or grey. The waistcoat is of a matching material, or possibly lighter, and is worn with striped trousers, also of a serge. He will then have a silk cravat and a silk top hat. One of the King's influences has been the introduction of the Homburg hat, a felt hat with a small depression in the crown and a turned up silk-bound brim. As summer approaches the Boater can be worn; and can often be seen at events such as the Henley Regatta.

For evening wear too the dress code is strict: a black dress coat, with tails, white waistcoat and trousers that match the coat. If one is dining at home or at a men's club the tailed jacket is more like a lounge suit. The latter item is very popular with King Edward, who also brought us the Norfolk jacket. This is of tweed and is usually in what is considered rather "loud" colours.

Essential for evening wear are gloves. While tan kid gloves can be worn in the daytime, suede is recommended for the evening. Finally, a silk scarf should be worn.

Of particular importance to my husband is his pocket-watch, given to him by his father. Charles's is a very fine silver, full-hunter. This means that the watch glass has a metal cover to protect it. The watch chain is an integral part of the watch and should be seen outside the waistcoat, whilst the watch itself is placed in a pocket on the opposite side. Nor is Charles ever to be seen without his pipe or tobacco pouch, which he keeps in his coat pockets.

Overcoats are an essential part of the man's wardrobe and quite a number prove very popular. The Chesterfield, the Ulster and the Raglan are all much in evidence. Charles's favourite is his Raglan. This is a long coat, waterproof and has side seams to give access to the pockets. It is ironical that the coat made popular and famous by Lord Raglan has been remembered, whereas the senseless slaughter that occurred during the Crimean War has all but been forgotten.

Paris fashion models arriving in Britain, 1907.

The dandy, though not a person I have much occasion to meet, is nevertheless part of society and can be observed in all the newspapers and magazines. Flamboyant dress is the order of the day for such men, who sport velvet collars, brightly coloured ties and gloves and perhaps a hat tipped at a rakish angle. They are not all of aristocratic background – many are artists and actors. Lord Randolph Churchill and Joseph Chamberlain

Henley Regatta, 1910.

are often called "dandies" for their sartorial elegance. Chamberlain became famous for his silk hats and monocle but most notably for the orchid he wears in his buttonhole, or, to give it the proper name, *boutonnière*.

The most notorious dandy is Oscar Wilde, with his love of velvet cloaks and silk cravats, brightly coloured tweed trousers and his small bowler hat tipped rakishly over his brow. Charles and I are never at ease

with this kind of dressing – it's all a little too vulgar.

King Edward was ever keen to keep up appearances and was often heard to rebuke people within his circle for not dressing correctly: even the Marquis of Salisbury suffered at the King's hands when he appeared in a somewhat dishevelled state. The marquis had to admit according to a source at the time, that *"It was a dark morning, and I am afraid that at the moment my mind must have been occupied by some matter of less importance."*

It seems he had rushed to get dressed without the services of his valet.

I have dwelt upon those ladies and gentlemen who can afford to have valets and a retinue of other staff to look after their clothes and to help them dress. This is not the case for all. Many families have to do their own washing and mending, and purchase clothes that are inexpensive. I allow myself one small luxury, which is to change my outfit before receiving any visitors in the afternoon. It is customary for visitors to be received between

All dressed up and ready for Ascot.

~ *An Edwardian* Housewife's Companion ~

three o'clock and five o'clock and for the husband to be out of the house. For this I am able to don what is known as the tea gown. This is a little more frivolous than my formal day wear. It is often made of the softest silks and laces and one of the benefits is that it does not have to have a corset structure, therefore allowing much more freedom of movement and the opportunity to relax a little more.

Washing fine silks and laces has to be undertaken with extreme care, so the following advice may be well worth observing for those who have

Playing "diabolo" on the beach.

to wash garments themselves or need to explain to staff how it should be done properly.

The Best Methods for Washing Silk and Cambrics

Lingerie blouses are becoming as hygienic as they are dainty, but alas they are costly possessions and will have to be constantly sent to a laundry. Why not wash them at home? Get a piece of good clean soap, Primrose is perhaps best, and some boiling water, which must be allowed to cool a little. Then make a soapy lather. Shake first your cambric and muslin blouses so that they are free of dust and put them into the lather and kneed and squeeze them but be sure to avoid rubbing them. Rinse them in two basins of hot, clean water and then a basin of cold water. If the blouses are white they must be rinsed in bluing water. Then put through the wringer very carefully, use hot thin starch and iron them on the right side. Should they be embroidered they should be ironed on the wrong side over a flannel so as not to bring out the pattern. Organdie blouses may be laundered in the same fashion, but organdie or cambric blouses with coloured, oriental or flowery patterns should be washed with rice that has been boiled for some time and then rinsed in two clean rice waters.

We live in a period of excess and extremes, and many people are concerned by the costs and are always looking to spend wisely and not to waste

A fine display of Edwardian hats.

anything unnecessarily. I hope you will take as much delight as I did in reading this article about the re-use of old stockings.

> ### One Use for Old Stockings
>
> *Few English people know that an important English industry depends upon the supply of the Russian peasant's old stockings.*
>
> *An English woollen manufacturer, visiting Russia some time ago on the look out for Russian wool, noticed that the long stockings worn by the peasants were made of particularly fine wool. This wool is spun by the women in their homes. The idea struck him that the old worn-out stockings might be utilised in his mill, and he proceeded to buy up all he could get. In many of the Russian villages now the old stockings are collected by agents and forwarded to the great fair at Ninji-Novgorod, which is held annually in July and August. These old stockings are eagerly bought up by certain English woollen mills, where by elaborate machinery they are torn into shreds and thoroughly washed and purified before going through the usual process of the weaving mills.*
>
> *Finally the old worn-out stockings emerge as fine cloth for costumes, soft white blankets and other dainty woollen goods.*

It may have crossed your mind that as our dress is so cumbersome it must also be extremely hot. I can testify to the fact that this is so. Therefore the occasional use of scent may be necessary. The most popular and my particular favourite is violet; there are others such as Jordan's water and Atkinson's lavender, as well as rose and orris root. I cannot envisage your needing to discuss matters of perspiration, but if you do then I suggest a French phrase, "*bouquet de*

corsage", which I think you will agree sounds a little gentler on the ear.

I hope you have found my thoughts on fashion useful. I conclude by recommending that you read the newspapers and journals to keep abreast of the latest fashions so that you do not fall behind — and also so that ladies who run businesses such as my own can keep working hard to create the designs that you all desire.

These ladies are all wearing the very latest fashion, the "long coat".

Recreation

Entertainment in the home could consist of a family gathering around the piano for a sing-a-long or, for those better off, listening to a gramophone record, then just coming into vogue. In addition to trips to theatres and music halls, cinema was beginning to appear in the latter half of the decade. Buffalo Bill was going around the country with his *Wild West Show*, and Gertie Millar and Little Tich were on stage.

Edwardian ladies and gentlemen take a stroll along the sea front.

There is so much to keep one entertained today. The whole family can enjoy a sing-a-long around the piano, or a trip to the theatre. The formal dance or party is only for adults, but entertainment may be had teaching the growing child what to expect when they are old enough to attend such functions.

In Bradford we are lucky to have a number of galleries and museums to visit, and do so as often as time allows. Close to where we live Cartwright Hall has recently been opened (Charles and I were in fact invited to attend the opening, and what a day that was!). The Prince and Princess of Wales led the opening ceremony, which formed part of an exhibition held in Lister Park. A large pavilion was erected where displays of all types were shown – there was even a Somalian village recreated and a water chute to ride down, which the children adored.

One should take every opportunity one can to visit these places, since they contribute to not only your own education, but also to your children's.

An early Mercedes motor car, c.1901.

The Formal Occasion

If you move in higher circles then you must take note of the London season, as it is known. You will notice if you are in the metropolis that many of our "colonial cousins", Americans, will be in town. These wealthy individuals are keen to enter the highest echelons of British society and seem determined to ingratiate themselves there, particularly those of aristocratic and noble disposition – however, I digress.

I have chosen some highlights of the London season that I hope will be of interest. May sees the opening of the Royal Academy Exhibition, a chance to see all the latest designs in dresses and the like from across the

The 1909 Wright Flyer.

world. I take particular interest in the newspaper reports of this exhibition so that I can see and anticipate what my ladies will be asking for in the following months. June brings Derby Day and Ascot week, where one can again see the finest costumes. August sees the Henley Regatta and Cowes week and the Goodwood race meeting. Those who enjoy their shooting will, of course, head off to the country for the "glorious 12th" for the start of the grouse-shooting season.

The tea dance is a favourite of mine. Charles and I will attend as many as time will allow, as they are far removed from the strictures of formal parties where one has to observe the restrictive etiquette expected of that type of function.

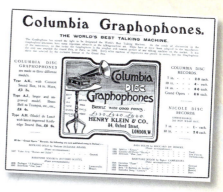

Unlike a formal ball, tea dances are held in the afternoon or early evening. For those who enjoy dancing, like myself, tea dances give the opportunity to dance regularly. There are new dances being introduced all the time and this is the place to learn them, accompanied by an orchestra. Whilst I am a little uneasy in the company of some Americans, their music is undoubtedly exciting. The current style is called ragtime and its most famous exponent at present is Scott Joplin, with his tune 'Maple Leaf Rag'.

Balloon race c.1906.

One does not just have to listen to the music whilst at a dance, one can also purchase sheet music and play it at home – if you are lucky enough to have a piano. Charles and I received a piano as a wedding present from his parents, and I often retire to the drawing room to play the new melodies. Charles is less enthusiastic, claiming such music is a little too "decadent". Not all dances are to my taste either; the Argentine Tango, for example, is too explicit for us. Younger girls may feel comfortable with them, and are of course at liberty to try them.

Tea dances are not very popular with the older generation, mainly because of the style of dancing that has become popular – in fact they are seen by some as rather risqué and to be left to the younger ones.

Theatre is our greatest love, and we are well served in our city and surrounding area. The music hall is not the sort of theatre we tend to visit, since this is a more working-class entertainment, a little less refined one might say, in that one is encouraged to join in with some of the songs and whilst some do have a jolly tune they can be rather bawdy at times and not suitable for refined ladies.

**An entrant in the 1906
New York to Paris rally.**

Launching the liner *Mauritania*, September 1906.

Yet these variety shows attract many hundreds of people and are extremely popular, featuring such stars as Vesta Tilley, who much prefers dressing as a man or boy for her act, and Marie Lloyd whose act is very dubious indeed and definitely not one I nor any member of my circle of friends would wish to attend. She is adored across the country for what can only be described as rather saucy lyrics, along with the strangest winks and gestures. I would like to say at this point that I do have some admiration for Miss Lloyd because she supported the strike by music hall workers over pay and hours.

Passengers from a stranded ferry are carried ashore at Calais, 1909.

"We can dictate our own terms. We are fighting not for ourselves, but for the poorer members of the profession, earning 30 shillings to £3 a week. For this they have to do double turns, and now matinées have been added as well. These poor things have been compelled to submit to unfair terms of employment, and I mean to back up the federation in whatever steps are taken." – Marie Lloyd, 1907

The famous tenor Enrico Caruso talks to a telegraph operator in 1909.

One performer we all delight in seeing is Henry Relph, better known as "Little Tich". At only 4 feet 6 inches tall, he performs a hilarious dance which he calls "The Big Boot Dance", wearing boots 28 inches long.

I would like to mention a music hall star from Bradford, Gertie Millar. She has starred in many productions across the country and is a favourite with women and men alike. Sadly, her husband, the music hall songwriter Lionel Monckton, found that dealing with the many men who also adore her was too much, and he eventually left her in 1905 following the tragic incident when a German gentleman and admirer broke into her boudoir and committed suicide.

As I have said, music hall is not really for the likes of us and we much prefer good theatre, preferably drama. Charles and I often visit the Theatre Royal on Manningham Lane in Bradford. But here, too, another tragedy struck. In October 1903 Sir Henry Irving collapsed on stage whilst performing in *Beckett*, uttering the final words "*into thy hands O Lord, into thy hands*". We were watching him at the time and found it most upsetting. He managed to return to his hotel but once again collapsed and died shortly after.

A church outing to Barnard Castle, 1906.

Aviator Samuel
Franklin Cody and
his wife prepare for
take-off.

George Alexander and Irene Vanbrugh on stage, 1908.

I do hope you have a more enjoyable experience at the theatre than we seem to have had recently.

Some of you may have been fortunate to witness the travelling show of Mr William Frederick Cody, better known as "Buffalo Bill". We were able to see the show on the outskirts of Bradford and watched as they re-enacted scenes from the "Wild West" such as *Custer's Last Stand*, and *Riding the Pony Express*. We were even treated to *Sitting Bull* himself and a band of 20 Indians. You will be able to see Miss Annie Oakley display her amazing shooting skills; there are performers from across the world including Cossacks and Turks, Mongols and Arabs all dressed in their colourful costumes.

I must add one final detail and tell you that one of my staff was lucky enough to meet "Buffalo Bill". Thomas Lister, a signalman on the railways and husband of Lillian, who works for me in the shop, took charge of getting the whole entourage into the city. There were three carriages to sort out and Thomas made all the arrangements for the smooth passage of the train and its passengers. There had been severe storms on the Monday when the show was originally planned and so it had to be postponed until the Tuesday, thus making the new arrangements particularly difficult. Mr Cody, alias "Buffalo Bill", was made aware of the efforts of this young man and wanted to meet him to express his thanks. Lillian and Thomas met him and had their photograph taken shaking hands with "Buffalo Bill" no less.

He takes his show across the country so I am sure you will be able to see a performance wherever you live.

Guests arriving by carriage for Derby Day, 1906.

Children's Fun

Children naturally enjoy parties, and whilst they do not need the formality of their adult equivalents, it is worth remembering some of the games they may like to play.

Blow Football, Blind Man's Buff and Pin the Tail on the Donkey are

Heading down Oxford Street on the bus, 1909.

Claude White, aviator, lands his plane at Ranleigh, 1910.

the favourites of most children, along with a game of Snakes and Ladders. The simplest games are sometimes the most successful, and a game of tag, leapfrog or hopscotch can be played. If you have a garden large enough why not try a game of croquet? One outdoor game that has recently been introduced is a horse-racing game. You set up a row of posts and blindfold one child, who in turn is led by another child with reins around the blindfolded child, and the winner is the child who is fastest around the course. Do be wary however of allowing the children to become overexcited, particularly the boys, as it is very hard to calm them down.

What sort of food to serve at a children's party is not a difficult decision. All children will enjoy sandwiches, cold meats, biscuits and cakes. Drink can be kept simple since there is not a single child who does not like a glass of lemonade. The highlight, however, will always be the birthday cake. This can be decorated in a variety of ways. Most children will like an iced cake, but a simple fruit cake will suffice. The requisite number of candles to blow out must not be forgotten and care must be taken with this practice. My own daughter has never wished to blow her own candles out as she cannot bear the smell of the extinguished candle. The older child will enjoy cutting the cake, so a "guiding hand" should assist at all times.

Politics

From the early 1900s women became increasingly determined to secure the right to vote. There was disagreement on how best to achieve this goal between those advocating peaceful means and the more militant wing, led by the Pankhursts, which led to the foundation of the Women's Social and Political Union, soon to be known as the suffragette movement.

"All the world is changing at once." – Winston Churchill, 1911

Suffragettes targeted the post boxes as one of their many acts of vandalism.

David Lloyd George speaking at a rally in 1910.

THE WAYSIDE PLATFORM

ALL THE

GOOD PLANS

ARE MADE B

You may well be wondering why I am embarking on a subject which we ladies do not usually have either time or inclination to interest ourselves in. If I am honest, we are positively discouraged by our menfolk from troubling ourselves with thoughts of such high intellect and matters which really do not concern us. There is a home to run, there are children to supervise and educate and some of us have our own businesses and staff to attend to.

Charles, my dear husband, often asks why I read the papers in such depth. I often try to engage him in conversation about political matters not only within our own shores but also across the world. More disturbing still, to Charles, is my propensity to open discourse when at parties or gatherings of our friends. I do of course try to limit my thoughts and comments when I am with people I do not know well. But so much is happening within our own country that I find it hard not to have an opinion or the need to express it.

The most delicate matter, and one which I do have to be careful when discussing, is that of the suffragette movement. I can but admire what Emmeline Pankhurst and her followers are trying to achieve; yet their methods I find disturbing. But what else are they to do, when women are not being listened to? We are allowed to enter business, even set up our own as I have done, but we are not allowed to vote like the men. I am aware that many women do not possess the necessary intelligence for such important issues, and many are not interested. My own staff, for example, are never heard discussing politics, but concern themselves only with matters of a more domestic nature (and I clearly do not encourage them, since I wouldn't want them distracted whilst they work; they may

Children of striking Belfast dockworkers on a march.

Lady Constance Georgina Lytton participating in a march, 1909.

occasionally discuss a music hall act they have seen in one of our local theatres, but that is as far as they go).

This period has been one of major social and political reforms. Never have we seen the formation of so many political groups of all persuasions. I hear names used such as Anarchists, Nihilists and now we have Socialists as well. This group appeals to the working classes particularly, who are now beginning to feel they can affect changes in their favour. It has to be said that our parliament is certainly biased towards the upper classes and I often wonder if being wealthy is necessarily the best qualification for running the country.

"The sun never sets on the British Empire" is a phrase you will have heard many times, and so very true; but I fear things are changing dramatically across the globe and it is not always to our advantage. Our alliances across Europe are changing. Take for example Germany; the Kaiser is Queen Victoria's grandson and the King's nephew, but we are in a very uneasy situation with this country which now seems to be somewhat threatening in its stance towards other countries, not least our own.

I read with consternation the news reports of the Russo-Japanese War; a war over a port to which the Russians wish to have access for their fleet. Every day the papers are filled with accounts of the sea battles being won and the expectations of the Japanese Navy. I hold no particular opinion about either country, but I did notice the unrest the war created with the Russian people and their views on the Tsar and his government.

A war that is nearer to our hearts is the Boer War, which thankfully ended in 1902. My feelings are mixed regarding the conduct of the British during this time. Our country's actions towards the Boer people has led to much criticism across the world – I have even read the word "revulsion" in this regard. Because of the large number of prisoners taken, the British set up what are now called "concentration camps"; our government preferred to call them "camps of refuge". They included women and children not just soldiers. The treatment of prisoners was positively cruel in my eyes. Many were left to starve, illness was rife and the death rate increased dramatically. It is to be noted that there were separate camps for the black natives – and their plight was never really a matter of concern in the papers, nor for the British public it seemed.

Winston Churchill speaking at a rally in Manchester, 1909.

Of particular concern and interest to me was the humanitarian work of Emily Hobhouse. As a member of South African Women and Children's Distress Fund she visited many of the camps in January 1901 and returned to this country with her findings. She was considered a Boer sympathiser for highlighting the internee's plight. Emily spoke to Henry Campbell-Bannerman, leader of the Liberal Party and later to become British Prime Minister. He initially supported her cause but internal disputes within the Liberal Party stopped him pursuing the matter.

Over the next few months the papers were full of accusations and counter-accusations. Our government said the camps were "purely voluntary" and the Boer people were "contented and comfortable". Some of you may well remember David Lloyd George accusing the government of a "policy of extermination".

Emily's report caused much consternation among the politicians, and resulted in the Fawcett Commission in 1901. This was headed by Millicent Fawcett. Despite her being the leader of the women's suffrage movement she was a government supporter.

"It was late in the summer of 1900 that I first learnt of the hundreds of Boer women that became impoverished and were left ragged by our military operations. The poor women who were being driven from pillar to post, needed protection and organised assistance." – Emily Hobhouse

I have followed Emily's story very closely indeed and feel a certain empathy with her and her desire to do good for the people who get caught in wars in which they have neither influence nor control.

Her major concern was the women and children. Reports about their true plight were extremely vague. There was no official record of how many were interned. In fact Emily wasn't even sure how many camps there were. Initially she had thought there was only the one in Port Elizabeth. How wrong she was! She eventually discovered 34 camps. She was allowed to visit a number of them and to record the diabolical conditions she witnessed.

In some of the camps there were two and sometimes three families living in a tent. This could mean upwards of 12 people herded into the tiny space. Their suffering was compounded by the intense heat, unsuitable and limited food and poor hygiene facilities. In fact most families didn't even have access to a simple bar of soap.

The children suffered equally. Typhoid was rife because they were all getting what little water there was from filthy rivers, thereby increasing their risk. Children were wasting away through lack of food, their mothers doing everything within their power to keep them alive. How could the papers say that these camps were "havens of bliss"?

The suffering is unimaginable to you and me, and it was only Emily's reports that made us aware. I shudder to think how our nation was viewed around the world.

My husband tells me that the British Army needed to clear the villages so that order could be restored and that I should show more concern towards our own men.

Lancashire cotton mill workers locked out, 1910.

I quote once again from Emily's own words which I find describe this horror far better than I can:

"Above all one would hope that good sense, if not mercy, of the English people, will cry out against the further development of this cruel system which falls with crushing effect upon the old, the weak and the children."

The situation finally resolved itself by Lord Kitchener telling his commanders not to bring any more women and children to the camps but to leave them with the guerrillas, as they were called.

Women lawyers take part in a suffragette march, 1910.

VOTES FOR WOMEN

WE DEMAND THE VOTE THIS SESSION!

WOMENS SOCIAL AND POLITICAL UNION VOTES FOR WOMEN

All means of transport were used to promote *the cause*.

Madame Despard, an ardent campaigner for the cause of women's suffrage, visits No. 10 Downing Street.

"If Great Britain cannot win her battles without resorting to the despicable cowardice of the most loathsome cure on earth – the act of striking at a brave man's heart through his wife's honour and his children's life..." – Anon

I must now bring to your attention a discussion that has been not only in the papers but also in houses and businesses across the land and one which vexes Charles and I and many of our friends.

I am talking about the influx of aliens to our shores. I see reports every day about the number of people arriving from foreign lands to take up residence in this country and many, it would seem, are not the most desirable persons, being ill-educated and lazy. One only has to look at the crime reports in the papers to see many of those convicted are of this type.

It is my view that we need an Aliens Bill immediately to curb this influx. Such great efforts were put into the recent Brewer's Act so I cannot see why our politicians fail to follow a similar pattern and get this far more worthy and important act passed as soon as possible. I am a charitable person at heart and would welcome decent-living, clean and hard-working people, but not those we currently see on our docksides. Some see it as our duty

Women try on prison clothes to see what they might be wearing shortly.

to help and civilise these people, but I say charity begins at home. When we have achieved this state with our own people then we may begin to look abroad.

In this past decade we have seen four Prime Ministers. Our first, from 1885 to 1902, was the Conservative Robert Cecil, 3rd Marquis of Salisbury. He was followed by Arthur Balfour, from 1902 to 1905, also a Conservative, and then came the Liberal landslide election of 1905 putting Henry Campbell-Bannerman in power. Unfortunately he was never in good health and decided to resign in April 1908, which allowed Herbert Asquith to take over.

Robert Cecil was born in 1830 and educated at Eton and Christ Church, Oxford. A supporter of the Conservative Party, he was elected to represent Stamford in 1853. As Lord Cranborne, the title he inherited on the death of his brother in 1865, he played an important role in the defeat of the Parliamentary Reform Bill proposed by William Gladstone in 1866. As I am sure you will be aware, there had been much debate in parliament over many years as to who should be entitled to vote.

Arthur Balfour, Conservative Prime Minister 1902–1905.

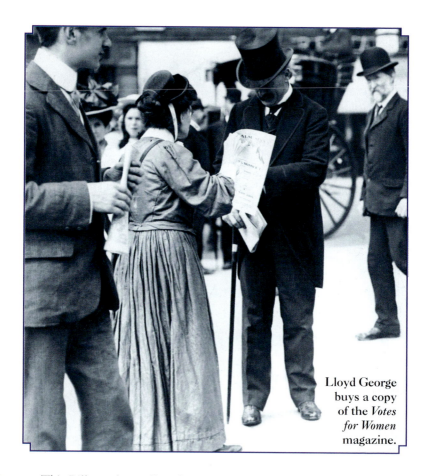

Lloyd George
buys a copy
of the *Votes
for Women*
magazine.

This Bill sought to allow those men with a certain income, which was a minimum 26 shillings a week, to be allowed a vote, thus avoiding giving any power to those considered unfit for the privilege. I often wondered why a poor man might be considered as unfit to vote. Cecil became leader of the Conservative Party in 1878 and finally Prime Minister in 1885. As he was a supporter of the policies that led to the Boer War I must say I was never quite at ease with him. He died in 1902.

Arthur James Balfour, nephew of Robert Cecil, took over from his uncle as Prime Minister in 1902. Whilst enjoying only a short time in office due to internal party disputes, the government resigning and the subsequent loss of the 1905 General Election, he nevertheless ushered in some major legislation. He was responsible for the Education and Irish

Land Reform Bills. He was also responsible for what became known as the *entente cordiale*, which established cordial relations with the government of France, thereby reducing the risk of war between our two countries. Balfour's government finally resigned and he lost his seat in the election that followed, but he did retain leadership of the Party.

Then in 1905 came the most dramatic General Election we have seen in many years. The Liberals swept to power and Campbell-Bannerman became Prime Minister. He was a Glaswegian by birth and had served in two of Gladstone's governments.

I have to declare a certain empathy with the man and to confess that, had I been allowed, my vote would certainly have gone to the Liberal Party. He spoke out against the concentration camps that had been established during the Boer conflict, which unfortunately created a rift within his own party. During his tenure he oversaw the granting of self-rule and government to South Africa in 1906 – or, to be specific, the region of the

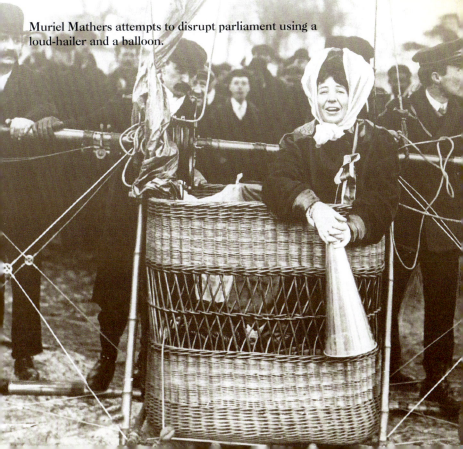

Muriel Mathers attempts to disrupt parliament using a loud-hailer and a balloon.

Transvaal and the Orange River Colony. But in 1908 he too had to resign because of ill-health, and died less than two weeks later.

Finally came Mr Herbert Asquith, a local man, born in Morley, which is less than 10 miles from our own home. Asquith had been Chancellor in Campbell-Bannerman's government in 1906.

Regretfully I must now declare my personal feelings towards Mr Asquith. These feelings are not pleasant ones, since he opposes women's suffrage. Along with many other women I felt anger towards a man who can decide how much tax we pay yet denies us the right to political representation. He suffers the wrath of the suffrage movement, with attempts to disrupt meetings he is speaking at. Asquith is not popular with women. Even when members of his own party entertain the idea that we should be granted the vote, he still opposes the idea. We all thought this was going to change during the 1910 General Election when he announced that if they were returned to power then women who owned property would be given a vote. Whilst not exactly what we wanted it was a move in the right direction; however, the despicable man changed his mind and brought legislation in that allowed *all* men the vote instead.

If there is one topic that can bring disharmony into the house it is the discussion of votes for women. Charles and I have spent many hours in heated discussion of this matter, which usually results in his retiring to his study to smoke a pipe and me trying to calm down and turn my attentions to something else.

Lloyd George in the dock being cross-examined by Christabel Pankhurst.

Sylvia Pankhurst at a rally in 1910.

I find it hard to see why women who are educated, intelligent mothers and business women are denied the right to say who governs the country and who sets legislation that affects us all. As I have pointed out on many occasions to Charles, I run a small business and employ people. I make all the necessary decisions regarding the staff; the purchase of materials, I deal with all the suppliers, I manage the finances and on top of that I run our home where again I employ the staff and make all the decisions on running our household. I am aware that Charles provides the finances and oversees them but I am more than capable of doing this myself, as Charles acknowledges.

From a woman's point of view this is the single most important political issue of the decade. But views differ on how our aims are to be achieved. Millicent Fawcett founded the National Union of Women's Suffrage

Christabel Pankhurst addresses a
meeting in Trafalgar Square.

Societies (NUWSS) in 1897, believing in peaceful protest. Her view is that any violence or vandalism will lose women any trust and respect they may have gained and will prevent their argument from being taken seriously. The issue seems to be whether women can be trusted with the vote, which I find a very disturbing view.

We are allowed on to the School Boards because many of us are business women – in fact some grander women were responsible for vast estates employing a large number of people such as gardeners and labourers and household staff. I reiterate that I myself employ three people and run a small but successful business. Millicent's argument is that women should be part of the process of law-making; we have to obey the laws but are not allowed to make them. I come back to the matter of paying tax: again we have no influence whatsoever.

Suffragettes get some sleep before a midnight meeting in Trafalgar Square, 1910.

Protesting women are arrested and led away.

Millicent Fawcett had my support very early on but I feel her methods are, at best, rather tame. There are a lot of meetings around the country, many speeches and demands are made; but still nothing happens. Millicent encourages women to speak at these meetings and even trains them for this very purpose. Her followers were keen on backing the male candidates in the 1906 election who said they supported women's suffrage. They also held regular meetings with politicians to discuss their cause and try to argue their case.

The women members of the NUWSS are what we would call middle class. They do not entertain any militant views but seek to change the law by peaceful means only. In fact when the issue arrived in parliament for debate in 1897 even Queen Victoria was opposed to women getting the vote.

Meanwhile, other women feel that the campaign needs more impetus and are prepared to ignore the "social graces" of NUWSS members. In 1903 Emily Pankhurst and her two daughters, Christabel and Sylvia, formed the Women's Social and Political Union – and what a difference this made! Their approach was so very different, and one I could not approve of at first since they were prepared to use violence to get what they wanted. They started off peacefully enough, but Emmeline's opinions changed when, following the death of her husband, she found out that a hall that was to be dedicated to her husband's name and used by the Independent Labour Party did not admit women.

The meaning of the word "suffrage" has changed these last years. Its original meaning was the "right to vote", but when Emmeline and her group became known as "suffragettes", the meaning altered to those prepared to use violence to obtain their goals. It was also at this time that Millicent Fawcett withdrew any support she had previously shown for the WSPU. They had worked together for some time but Emmeline's more radical approach did not suit Millicent and her party.

It was 1905 when the first major act of the party came to the public attention. Christabel Pankhurst and Annie Kenney attended a meeting in Manchester where two Liberal politicians, Winston Churchill and Sir Edward Grey, were speaking. The women constantly interrupted the speeches to ask if the politicians were in favour of giving women the vote. They were ignored by both men, and so the women finally unrolled a banner declaring "Votes for Women". Perhaps, like me, you are concerned

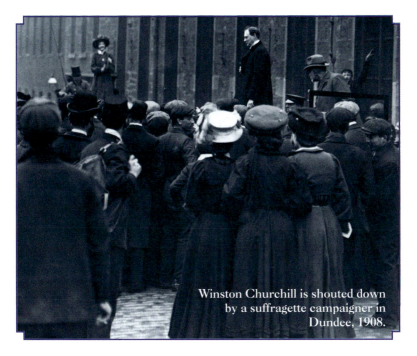

Winston Churchill is shouted down by a suffragette campaigner in Dundee, 1908.

Annie Kenney is led away under arrest after disrupting a political meeting, along with Christabel Pankhurst.

by this lack of respect shown to the politicians and to others attending the meeting; respectable people did not act in this manner. Even if you disagree with someone you keep silent. This was the height of bad manners, and both Christabel and Annie were forcibly removed from the building and charged with causing an obstruction and assaulting a police officer.

When they arrived in court they were asked to pay a fine. But they soon realised that their cause would gain far more publicity if they were to refuse and go to prison. "Deeds not words" became their slogan, and acts of violence and vandalism increased. Letter boxes were burnt, windows in Oxford Street were smashed, even churches were attacked because the Church of England opposed their aims; members chained themselves to the railings at Buckingham Palace and even hired boats to sail up the Thames and, as my beloved Charles declared to "barrack" Members of Parliament.

You will all know that putting these women into prison has led to many of them refusing to eat. The more they suffer the more the papers report their plight and, I suppose, the more publicity they gain by these acts. This was not a planned action. It was Marion Wallace who first took this course of action in 1909 and other members soon heard about her decision and took it upon themselves to follow suit.

I overheard a close friend say :

"Tea parties weren't going to do the trick but perhaps publicity and martyrdom just might."

Deeds not words. – Emmeline Pankhurst

Trust in god – she will provide. – Emmeline Pankhurst

Ability is sexless. – Christabel Pankhurst

It was so staid, so willing to wait, so incorrigibly leisurely. – Sylvia Pankhurst

Patience and trust were abandoned, and indignation and bitterness took their place: the old ways led nowhere, the old friends did nothing and it was time for a fresh enterprise. – Ray Strachey

Beauty has claims for which she fights
At ease with winning arms
The women who want women's rights
Want mostly women's charms. – Punch

To man belongs the kingdom of the head: to woman the empire of the heart. In every pure and legitimate relation – as daughter, sister, wife, mother – woman is the direct assistant of individual man. – James McGrigor Allan

Dressed for Ascot.

~ A Guide for THE PERFECT HOME ~

"An Edwardian lady in full dress was a wonder to behold, and her preparations for viewing were awesome". William Manchester

The fear I have is, lest we should invite her unwittingly to trespass upon the delicacy, the purity, the refinement, the elevation of her own nature, which are the present sources of its power. – William Gladstone

As to the suffrage movement, it was gathering of people of all sorts, united by one simple idea, which necessitated the surrender of no prejudice or race or class. – Sylvia Pankhurst

Militant tactics were intended to expose men as the enemy and to make it clear what men were capable of doing to those they claimed to protect. – Dale Spender

Feminism is the whole issue, political enfranchisement a branch issue, and the methods, militant or otherwise, are merely accidentals. – Editorial in *The Freewoman*, 1911

One of the major drives behind feminism was the need felt by middle-class women to reassert their superiority of status over socially or racially inferior men to whom political and social change was bringing rights and thus status, which they were still denied. – R J Evans

Epilogue

Edward VII died at 11.45pm on 6 May 1910, having suffered a number of heart attacks. He was 68.

Despite his somewhat chequered reputation he took on his role as King with determination. He had travelled widely whilst heir apparent, and this experience was to prove invaluable in the following years. Many of the Royal Families of Europe were his relations, so he was well known and well aware of what was going on across the world; he became affectionately known as the "Uncle of Europe".

His mother had not been confident of her son's abilities, because of the various indiscretions that dogged his early years, but she was to be proved wrong. It was Edward's direct influence that brokered the improved relations between both France and Russia.

Edward VII's funeral procession passing through Windsor Castle.

He reigned over a period of sweeping social, political and economic transformations; the 1902 Education Act led to subsidised secondary school education, and many other Acts were passed specifically to help children; 1908 saw the introduction of the old age pension and 1909 saw the Labour Exchanges Act, which paved the way for national health insurance. When David Lloyd George, then Chancellor of the Exchequer, introduced the controversial "People's Budget" to pay for the Liberal government's programme of social reform, Edward became embroiled in a constitutional crisis. He was asked by Prime Minister Herbert Asquith to increase the number of Liberal peers to help counter Conservative opposition to the budget. Though eventually agreeing to comply with Asquith's request, he died during the consequent crisis.

Yet despite the myriad developments of these years, his reign had been a relatively peaceful one. The Boer War ended in 1902, and the King's unease at Germany's emerging power, though prescient, was not yet unravelling into the devastating consequences that were to come in the following decade.

"The lost golden age... all the more radiant because it is on the other side of the huge black pit of war." – J B Priestley

THE END